Life Lessons on the Sierra Trail

40 Years' Experiences in the John Muir Wilderness

Allen Clyde

CRAVEN STREET

B O O K S

Fresno, California

Illustrations by Claudia Fletcher

Cover photograph: *Packer with Mules on Tuolumne River Trail.*
Photo by Don Paulson / Jaynes Gallery / DanitaDelimont.com
Book design by Andrea Reider

Published by Craven Street Books
An imprint of Linden Publishing
2006 South Mary Street, Fresno, California 93721
(559) 233-6633 / (800) 345-4447
CravenStreetBooks.com

Craven Street Books and Colophon are trademarks of
Linden Publishing, Inc.

ISBN 978-0-941936-04-0

135798642

Printed in the United States of America
on acid-free paper.

Library of Congress Cataloging-in-Publication Data on file.

This is a modern-day parable based on true events, places, and people. Many of the individuals' names have been either changed or eliminated for the sole purpose of protecting the guilty.

—Allen Clyde

CONTENTS

Allen Clyde on horseback with packhorse

Foreword

The book you are holding is an awesome read! It will enrich your life! Dr. Allen Clyde, a master storyteller and wilderness expert, will take you on an unforgettable ride through the high Sierra wilderness, a ride on which you will experience the grandeur of the majestic Sierras and learn vicariously the skills of high-country horse packing.

You will be exposed to the thrilling wonders and rigors of the magnificent John Muir Wilderness. Throughout these action-packed scenarios you will learn what it is to ride hard, learn crucial lessons equipping you for the challenges of life, and laugh out loud often as you become acquainted with the skills of horsepacking and meet unique and colorful characters, mostly pleasant, and some not so. Dr. Clyde held me captive from page one to the end, and left me wanting more. You are on the right trail!

—Jack Hannah, teacher, coach, singer, song writer, cowboy

Prologue

Yolanda was worried about her son Pablo. He was a good boy and never got into any serious trouble. He had just turned eighteen years old and was feeling more independent by the day. The friends he had been hanging with were turning toward the bad, and one had already been arrested. So far, Pablo had been able to avoid getting involved with any gang, but his friends hadn't.

Yolanda knew bringing him up here from Mexico when he was ten years old was the best choice for him, but she feared that if Pablo went with a gang, all would be for nothing. Pablo had done extremely well in school and had gotten accepted at California State University, Fresno. She hoped her son would follow through and attend college, but lately she was hearing him talk of not going and taking another path. As a child growing up in their poor village down south, Pablo had spent all his spare time on horseback with his uncles. She had never seen him far from horses since the age of four. He had spent days on end riding and enjoying every minute of it. But up here, in the center of the city of Fresno, Pablo felt somewhat lost and incomplete. He had immersed himself in schoolwork, but lately that focus was waning.

Yolanda worked hard all day as a house cleaner, and her feet were paying the toll and torturing her every step. She was glad her primary care doctor had set up an appointment with Dr. Clyde, a foot specialist.

Yolanda arrived at the office ten minutes early and was captivated by the pictures on the waiting room wall. Each one had an image of a horse in it. Many had high-country scenes, and others were of rodeo bronc riders. Right on time, Yolanda was led into an exam room. Along the way, she had noticed similar pictures on display in the rooms she passed.

Within a minute, Dr. Clyde entered, introduced himself, and sat on a stool near her feet. Yolanda described her foot issues, and Dr. Clyde explained her treatment options and went to work on her feet. She felt compelled to ask him about all the horse-related pictures in every room. He looked up, smiled, and told her about his nonprofit rodeo program and his forty years of outfitter-guiding in the John Muir Wilderness east of town. Soon he changed the subject and asked about her and her family.

Yolanda first spoke of her eldest son, Pablo, and his plans to go to Fresno State in the fall and her hope that he would follow through. This caught Dr. Clyde's attention. He mentioned that he was on the Fresno County Board of Education and wanted to know more about Pablo's ambitions. She said that he was a good student but unsure about his future goals. She divulged that this was a confusing time for Pablo. Dr. Clyde then asked about his main interests, thinking they might give her son some direction. She said that he had spent his childhood totally absorbed in horses in the mountains back home in Mexico and how much he missed that life. She added that Pablo had no regrets about coming up to California, since his education had been top-notch, but now that he had turned eighteen, he was faced with decisions.

"Maybe he needs to go someplace else for the summer," Dr. Clyde suggested. "Get away from his so-called friends and maybe afterward see the world in a different light. I guess him traveling out of the country is not an option due to finances." Yolanda nodded her head in agreement. "How about having him come by the office so we can talk when my wife, Deb, is here. I have an idea that might work for everyone. We need a rider, and he needs to get out of Dodge for a while."

Two weeks later, Yolanda dropped Pablo off at Clyde's mountain pack station to start work. Pablo was full of apprehension and anticipation. He knew about horses, but beyond that, the learning curve was just beginning.

CHAPTER 1

Outward Bound

"Wake up, Pablo. It's already 5:00 a.m. and the sun beat ya," Clyde yelled. Pablo opened one eye and the other soon followed. The small lodgepole pine cones he saw out the window were still, indicating a calm and clear day ahead.

Pablo shuffled into the cookhouse where Clyde already had the cowboy coffee to a rolling boil. He had added one coffee cup of cold water to settle the grounds. He poured his cup and the one Pablo presented. "Meet ya at the corral," Clyde said, "after I take Deb her coffee." This was his ritual every morning while she was still in bed. With just a small amount of cream, no sugar, but a sprinkle of love he always told her as he set the cup on the small table beside her.

"Which way are we headed today?" Pablo asked.

"We're going to the Niche again with a load of resupply for Outward Bound," Clyde answered. "Looks like five packhorse loads, all tight and heavy as usual. We'll take the youngest horse, July, and put him in the training position, right behind the lead packhorse. Should get along just fine. This being his second trip this summer, the four hours in and four out shouldn't be any trouble for him today. Go ahead and put packsaddles on Nevada, Pearl, Poco, and Loper to finish the string. Saddle Jay for yourself and I'll ride Harley today."

The typical resupply loads for Outward Bound always go in duffel bags and one large plastic bag. Three to five cans of stove

Pablo

fuel were packed separately. Clyde and Pablo filled the two canvas-leather bags (sometimes called panniers) for each horse and placed them in the back of the flatbed. Ten pack loads in all. Then came the five lash ropes and five canvas top tarps.

About then, Deb hollered out the backdoor, "Frying the eggs," letting them know she was on the last step and breakfast would be put on the table in only a few minutes. Pablo had learned it was better not to be late, or he would catch hell if the food got cold. It was always a gesture of respect to be in before breakfast was completely ready. That way he could help finish setting the table and get milk and cups out.

The horses were saddled, so this was a good time to stop for breakfast anyway. As Clyde and Pablo walked to the cookhouse, the two dogs, Dinkey and Patsy, followed partway, then stopped and returned to their usual sitting spots next to the horses, in the

4

Dinkey and Patsy

morning sun. Experience told them since the horses were tied up and had saddles on, Clyde and Pablo would soon return. Breakfast consisted of bacon, fried potatoes with onions, peppers, two eggs each, and toast. The lunch burritos had been prepared ahead of time. After taking their dirty dishes to the sink and depositing a burrito into their vest pockets, Clyde and Pablo went out to the hitching rail. The dogs started tail-wagging back and forth, making a fan mark in the dirt.

Clyde opened the stock trailer gate and walked in with the first horse, Nevada. She was always OK to be up against the front trailer wall. No problem for her, but many would not tolerate this and would push back, only to take up three horse spaces in the front. Pablo put in the rest of the string one at a time—Loper, Poco, Pearl, then July. All alternated head to tail. This was more comfortable for the horses and packed them in tighter. Not only can you get more horses in the trailer, but when they go around turns leaning against each other doesn't bother them after they get used to it. Then came Jay and Harley.

"OK, Dinkey, time to load up," Clyde commanded. He didn't have to remove a side panel, for Dinkey jumped, flat-footed, up and over into the bed. "Patsy, you need to stay and keep Deb company today. Your turn next trip." Clyde knew all along that Dinkey would go on three out of four trips since Patsy was getting old. But he figured she would forget he said that by tomorrow. Pablo was always amazed that Patsy seemed not to care. She simply walked back to the porch to assume the usual position.

They waved to Deb as they went by the cookhouse and called on the radio. "We're out the gate. See ya about 6:00," Clyde said.

"Be careful," Deb answered back.

Hauling up the six-mile road to Courtright Lake's Maxson trailhead takes about thirty minutes. The trip is slow going with seven horses and a curvy road. They go across the single lane over the dam and finally to the spike station, the staging area to start a pack trip. This is the departure and end point for all areas east of Courtright Lake into the John Muir Wilderness. These areas include Red Mountain Basin, Blackcap Basin, Bench Valley, and the North Fork of the Kings River. After backing in, as always leaving the parked truck pointing in the direction of home, they unloaded the horses and tied them to hitching rails.

"Let's load up Poco, Pearl, Loper, and Nevada first, July last," Clyde said. They did so, then put on top tarps to protect the loads from dust and the elements, and then tied it all down with box-hitch-knotted lash ropes. After this, they lined up the horses, Pearl first, then July followed by the other three.

"Always best to load the greenest horse last. Gives them less time to get restless and into trouble. Pablo, put the quietest load on her. Less for her to worry about too," Clyde said.

Pablo knew how to tie the string together. The fifteen-foot lead rope goes under a spider strap on the rear breeching, under the left bag load, and around the neck secured with a bowline knot. You want the lead line to be just barely long enough so the horses can drink. If the rope is any longer, it will get between the hind legs of the horse in front of them. Some horses will tolerate this, but others will start bucking big time. With July in the second place and double lead lined, one on each side, he couldn't get around either side and would learn to stay in line and not cause trouble.

"You'll notice, Pablo, all the lead ropes have what are called panic snaps. They allow a quick release in the event of any trouble. Knots fuse hard if the horse jerks back, and you're never able to untie them in a hurry. Saved a lot of horses' lives and equipment over the years with these snaps," Clyde quietly professed.

After all was set, lunches in saddlebags, and water bottles filled, Clyde said, "OK, Pablo, you lead the string this time. Hold the lead rope in your hand. Never get lazy and tie off to the saddle horn. I've known several people who almost got killed trying this. Don't coil the rope around your hand either. That's a good way to lose fingers or your whole arm if he jerks back and bolts for what ever reason. Keep to an easy slow walk at first, then pick up only slightly. You can only go as fast as the slowest horse anyway. You'll notice I put the most experienced horses in the back. When we get to tight turns in the trail, you'll see why. Remember, always slow down on all turns, rocks, creeks, or any other trouble spots. The fastest way to lead a pack string is slowly."

During the first couple hundred yards, Pablo turned around in the saddle numerous times and noticed how calm things were. Even July settled in, seeming to get the idea that being less fidgety meant less work. Strange how the horse picked up the routine just from being around the other, more experienced animals.

Knowing what he was thinking, Clyde remarked, "See, the smart ones learn fast. Don't let up looking back to keep an eye on the string. Best to spot potential trouble before it develops into a serious wreck. Head on a swivel goes for a lot of things in life."

The chickadees let Pablo know he was in their 'hood as he rode by. They alerted the golden-mantled ground squirrels of the invaders. The horses gave only passing interest to the racket, as did Dinkey. Dinkey, a crossbreed McNab and Black and Tan hound and a working cattle dog, learned long ago that chasing squirrels was a waste of time and energy. Not enough caught for the amount of effort.

They crossed two small streams and then went up a mild grade filled with granite. Pablo was always amazed at how sure-footed these mountain horses were. Clyde had told him ranch-raised horses grew up knowing how to walk on the rocks.

"These horses don't know what flat country is," Clyde had said. "When they stop rolling downhill after being born, the little buggers have to walk back uphill to get their first nursing. Why, if I put them all out on flat country, they would just stand there, bug eyed and confused. Yeah, letting them grow up only in the mountains keeps the body and feet in top shape. Traveling in 10,000-foot high country all day is no big deal to 'em. That's why these top-shelf athletes have my utmost respect. I give 'em a salute every day. Won't be long and you'll feel the same way."

California
Gray Squirrel

Claudia Fletcher
2020

After about an hour and a half they topped the grade at the Hobler Lake turnoff and started the descent to Long Meadow. As they rode the trail next to the open meadow and creek, Clyde pointed out, "Pablo, look up and see that granite ridge up on the skyline. That all is the Le Conte Divide. This side is the John Muir Wilderness and over that is Kings Canyon National Park. Joseph Le Conte was a geologist and natural history professor at the University of California. He explored this Kings River area extensively and was a founding member of the Sierra Club. Look up to the left and ya see a large granite peak. That's Mount Henry. In fact, Mr. Le Conte named it after Joseph Henry. I guess Joseph Henry was quite

John Muir Wilderness Sign

a guy too. Died in the late 1800s. He taught at Princeton and was a founding member of the Smithsonian Institution. I hear he also was a founding member of the National Weather Service."

After about an hour riding down a gentle descent, they crossed a major stream called Post Corral Creek. Pablo observed how calmly the rear horses waited while the front horses drank. Then, after slowly moving the string up, allowing the rear ones to drink, the front horses simply stood still. When the horses were done, the group moved up the trail. This was when things got steep. Tiptoeing up over the granite, the lead lines stayed slack. "That speed is just right, Pablo. Never get in a rush. Much faster that way," Clyde said.

The views got more fantastic as Clyde and Pablo climbed higher. Soon they were walking out on granite bluffs with sheer drop-offs. Pablo was getting a cold sweat, but his horse, Jay, never flinched, calming Pablo greatly. Jay never paid much attention to

Sign for Blackcap and Kings River

either side; he simply put one hoof in front of the other. He sometimes stretched a step to get over a log or rock on the trail, then slowed down to let the string do the same.

"Pablo, every time you have to slow down by half a step, you have to do the same for each horse in the string. If your saddle horse takes a half step, every horse tied behind ya also needs to take one. Five packhorses total three steps on the slow down. That's why the more turns or step-overs along the trail, the longer it takes to get anywhere. Remember to stay slow until the last horse is past the problem. That's not only smart but mighty considerate. Horses will learn to respect ya for it. There's not a drop of water up this grade to the top, so it was a good thing to water up the horses back at the creek. We won't get another chance until we get back here on the return," Clyde said.

After about four hours, the Niche came into view. The Niche was about 9,400 feet and a reasonably flat spot to rendezvous with Outward Bound for their resupply. It's the last time the Post Corral Creek drainage can be seen, and the first time Red Mountain Basin comes into view.

At this gorgeous viewpoint Clyde and Pablo met the hikers waiting for resupply. The hikers numbered about twenty. After unloading the ten pack loads, folding the tarps, and rolling up the ropes, Clyde

White Pine

said to Pablo, "Go mosey around and talk to these kids. Most are your age, and you will be surprised where they're from."

"Hi, I'm Pablo, where are ya from?" he asked a small group standing next to a white pine.

"Joe here is from New York, I'm David and from Chicago, Sally here is from Detroit, and Lil is from Los Angeles. We will be seniors next year in high school. Been on the trail about ten days now. Getting low on food and sure glad to see you," David said as they all knelt down to inspect the new delivery. "Wow, apples, oranges, raisins, celery, onions, carrots, just look at all this cool stuff." Pablo was surprised. He thought they would only get excited about candy bars but not at all. These kids were practical.

As usual, Dinkey was a big hit. With her direct, calm manner, she would walk up and sit right on the foot of a chosen admirer. Then she would look up perfectly still with her hound face and direct stare, unwilling to move or flinch until petted. This act never failed. The young hikers gravitated around her. Dinkey was clearly in her element and loving every minute. Seems the hikers had pets at home that they dearly missed and Dinkey filled that neglected void.

Pablo was envious. All the pretty girls just flocked around Dinkey as if she were a magnet. He vowed quietly to himself, "I should get a dog."

"What you muttering to yourself now?" Clyde said.

"Just admirin' how that dog gets all the attention with so little effort. Doesn't seem fair," Pablo said.

"Well, no one in this world ever said life was fair. But that doesn't stop ya from learning by watchin'. She just walked up calm, not threatening them at all. Watch her directly staring straight into their eyes and not looking away. They can't resist petting her, and Dinkey knows it works every time. That's why she never misses an opportunity on the trail or here. The smart ones figure it out fast. Yep, that dog has more friends than you or I will ever have.

Kenja

"Now watch that young, fit, and trim African-American man over there. The surprising thing is he's not young. Old enough to be your dad.

"Name's Kenja. He's the leader, and everyone here respects him. Watch how he interacts with all the students, one at a time. Checks on 'em, then gently gives direction on what food they need to resupply and how to pack it. Gives them a thumbs-up, a smile, and moves on. He's been doing this for over twenty years and knows how to make progress. It's much better to gently lead from the front than to push hard from the back. Before you know it, they will be at the destination and proud of their accomplishment."

"There's over twenty kids here. How can he keep them all goin' and smilin'?" Pablo asked. "They're coming from big cities, so there has to be some that will tell him to kiss off after doing fifteen miles a day in this rough country and at 10,000 feet."

"Well, it usually works like this," Clyde said. "After a short time, there is always a few of these young kids who pick up on Kenja's lead and will do small acts of encouragement for the slower ones. First thing ya know, the whole group is on autopilot. All he has to do from then on is glance around once in a while, keep 'em headed in the right direction, follow along to make sure the group stays tight, and wear a smile. Now it's time to start reloading. These duffels will be repacked with trash, some unneeded food, empty cans of fuel and all.

"The leftover empty duffel bags can be folded up and put inside others to condense, and we can start refilling pack bags. There will be fewer of them and they'll be lighter. We'll put the heaviest loads on the youngest horses. The older ones have earned the right to take the lighter loads. Keep the string the same alignment as we came in. They got along just fine."

Pablo started with Pearl's loads, even on each side. Then he put the pack tarp on, tucking the front and rear of the tarp behind the pack saddle tree so it would stay visible from the front and back. That way he could quickly tell if anything was leaning from either end while they were riding. Then he threw the lash rope cinch with hook over the top. After walking around, he flipped the cinch hook strap back under the horse, walked around again to retrieve and hook the rope to pull it tight, and secured it with a half-hitch knot. Then he threw the rope back over the top.

Clyde was on the other side where he took the rope, made a loop around the front and then the pack to form the box hitch, pulled tight, and flipped the remaining rope back over the top to Pablo. He did the same and tied off on the top with two half-hitches. This took about seven minutes. Then on to the next one until all five horses were loaded. Since they were never untied from the string, all was good to turn around and start back.

"Before we head out, let's walk over and admire the scenery," Clyde said. After only about thirty yards, a whole new view came from behind the lodgepole pines. "There is the top of Red

Lodgepole Pine

Mountain. Only red at the very tip-top. Gets its color from the iron oxide. First climbed by Le Conte just before 1900. Just to the right and downslope is Hell For Sure Pass. That's where the trail goes and the boundary for Kings Canyon National Park. You're looking at over 11,000 feet up there.

"This whole area is called Red Mountain Basin and has about fourteen named lakes and probably twice that many that are unnamed. Over there is Fleming Mountain with Fleming Lake just below it. Running out of that is Fleming Creek. Mr. Fleming was a sheepherder in this area. Worked for a boss named Helms. Helms's name is all over this area, including the PG&E power plant we went over. Yeah, it's buried under the mountain we came over with the truck on our way here. I'll explain more on that later.

"Way over there is Mount Hutton. It's almost 12,000 feet. Named after James Hutton, who passed away just before 1800. Said to be the father of modern geology. Way around the corner to the left is a canyon that will lead up to Mount Henry, which you saw from Long Meadow. Way in the back is the top of Emerald Peak. It's about 12,500 feet high. I hear the top has a green hue. Can't see that from here, and it's a long way into the park.

"Imagine looking way around that corner. Far up the creek drainage are Lower and Upper Indian Lakes. Right behind them is Mosquito Pass. All the water from the top that goes this way goes into the Kings River. On the other side of the pass the water goes into the San Joaquin River and ultimately out to the Pacific Ocean. The top is the divide. Pretty cool, I mean literally. The air flows up from the valley in middle California and goes up the slope and funnels through these narrow passes. Standing up there, sometimes ya have to put rocks in your pockets to keep from blowing away. Let's go shake hands with Kenja and the hikers and get on our way."

After bidding a farewell, they set out back down the mountain, Pablo in the lead. "Remember Pablo, keep it slow and easy. Keep the same speed going down that we came up. We still have the same tight turns, rocks, logs, and creeks going down. They haven't moved.

Don't forget—slow, easy, and lead with a smile. Let the horses think it's their idea to keep moving. Always watch the lead ropes of each horse. If you have a little slack in each one, then you're going just right," Clyde said.

After about thirty minutes and past a rough patch of the trail, Pablo asked, "How did you come up with the names of these horses?"

"Well, that is a long story. You see, each is an individual, and a name should be given that has some meaning just for them. Take Pearl, for instance. The lead packhorse behind you. Named after Pearl Lake over in Blackcap Basin. You haven't been there yet. The lake is about 9,600 feet high. All rock and virtually not a tree in sight. Just granite and water. Her mother was named Blackcap. It's another way to keep track of the lineage. That big white blaze on her face against the sorrel body is a good way to recognize her in the herd. She'll always be a packhorse, though. Will carry a load all day without a care, but if ya try to get on her back she'd buck you up to the tree tops. Same as her mother.

"Now right behind her, as you know, is July. Only reason I named him that is that he was born in July, since I was running out of names. Then there is Loper, named after Loper Peak. John Loper was a cattleman from Ohio who came here in the 1800s. Then Poco—no reason—just wanted a horse by that name. Last is Nevada. Had to have a horse by that name after watching the movie *Nevada Smith*. Nice paint horse. Easy to spot in a group.

"My horse's name, Harley, came with the horse. Patient came in the office, said their daughter was going off to college, and wanted the horse to go to a good home. Asking price was $1,500. They had him for fifteen years, got 'em when he was two. I said, when ya get to five hundred call me. I've never paid more than that and wasn't going to start. Six months later they called me and said the horse was mine.

"When Deb and I went to pick him up, it was obvious the horse had spent most of those fifteen years in the corral. I had the daughter get on him. Harley didn't understand commands too well, but I could see that somewhere in his past there was a lot of training put in. I loaded him up and left.

"The mother said the daughter will have a hard time letting him go since she grew up with Harley. Well, I never heard a word from the daughter, but the mother was calling every couple of months to come and visit the horse. After telling her the horse was out on fifteen hundred mountainous acres with the whole herd and would take a whole day to gather in, she understood she would need to wait until the following summer. She finally came to Dinkey stable and spent about an hour hugging Harley. Still never heard from the daughter. I saw no reason to change the name. Took a year for him to relearn how to be a horse though. As it turns out, this sixteen hand black gelding was worth the trouble.

"Your horse, Jay, has an interesting story too. Named after a young man named Jay Hubbard. Worked here for about five years, then joined the county sheriff's office. You may remember the story, or at least your parents would. See, one of his brothers joined the Marines with a buddy and went to Iraq. Both were killed by an IED. Jay's youngest brother then wanted to join up. Jay said no way unless I go with you. They both went into the Army and off to Iraq. They were being transported in country in two helicopters, one brother in each, Army rule. Well, one of them goes down and all aboard were killed, including Jay's little brother. That was the end of Jay's Army career. They sent him home. One of those *Saving Private Ryan* type of things.

"Then the Army had a crazy rule that since he came home early, they wanted his signing bonus back and were going to take away his medical benefits. His wife was pregnant at the time. I think it was Congressman Nunes that got a bill put through that took care of the problem. Called it the Hubbard Bill. It was interesting to see Jay on national TV, testifying to all in Washington with his uniform on. I was just remembering all the times he rode with me on these very trails. Jay later told me the best job he ever had was up here in these mountains. Anyway, I always wanted a horse named after him. Got Jay from a trail guide out of Yosemite. This animal came knowing the mountains and how to get around."

As they descended the mountain, Post Corral Creek with its meadow came into view. "We'll water up here again and let the horses take a break," Clyde said. "Never knew exactly how this place got its name. Never saw any posts around. There was a guy named William S. Post of the US Geological Survey and a lake is named after him, but I don't know if there is any connection. Come over here to this rock a minute. See the brass disk. That's a benchmark. Indicates the elevation at this spot. Put there by the Survey back in 1951. Look close. See the three letters: J.R.H. That's James Ray Hedgpeth. He was the survey boss then. Put these benchmarks all over the mountains, not only here but the whole West, including Alaska. His family came here in the 1880s. Homesteaded a ranch next to mine down in the foothills. I leased his place for about twenty years until he passed away at almost ninety. His family then sold the place to me. Still running horses and cattle on it.

"His grandfather came here first. Was a roaming preacher. Had to settle on the higher foothills for a homestead, as the lower country was already taken up. Took twenty-five years living on various parcels to put it all together. He had a little shack, and when it came time to move, they numbered all the boards, put 'em on a wagon, and went over to the next parcel, and reassembled them. He settled in for another five-year stretch. Dug all the postholes by hand, sharpened

Benchmark

oak poles, and pounded them in with a large wooden mallet. They did have barbed wire. It was expensive, though, and they put in only two strands. A lot of work. Trust me, if metal T-posts were invented back then, you would never see a single wood post. But you make best use of what you have. Still true today."

As they rode on, paralleling Post Corral Creek, Clyde said, "Right around here, over by the creek, Deb found a lost hiker while she got her riders off the trail to rest. The hiker couldn't see the trail and was scared to death. Been away from her group all morning. Noticed she didn't have any socks and had big blisters on heels. Just tennis shoes over bare feet. Deb asked her where the socks were and all she got back was a blank stare. Didn't know. Had them on this morning.

"Well, Deb guided her back up on the trail and the girl took off up the trail toward me. Her group was camped on the same trail over at Hobler Lake. Yeah, she was about five miles from her group. I was way out ahead with the loaded packhorses. Deb radioed me with a heads-up. I slowed down, and when this hiker got to me, I made her stop and take her shoes off. I put on some medicine, accommodating padding, dressings, an extra pair of socks of mine. With her shoes back on she trotted on toward her group. All she had to do was stay on this obvious class-three trail. Thankfully, not only a guardian angel, Deb, came along but also me, a foot doctor. That was a lucky day for her.

"She was from a University of California, Santa Cruz, hiking class and got 180 degrees turned around just going out to pee. She then panicked and started to run. That explains all the scratches and scrapes on her face, hands, and legs. I radioed Deb and said all was good. Then radioed the US Forest Service to let them know the lost hiker was found and not to start a search. One was just getting started, since the group had sent out a runner, so we saved the county a lot of money.

"Lesson—stay together. It's amazing how many large groups let themselves get strung out for over a mile. The group leaders jackrabbit up the trail and let the less experienced hikers come along all separated. The slowest always end up dropping way in the back. They would then come up to a turn off and just have to guess. That's how some hikers get stuck out all night, become lost, and sometimes die. The fault is with the leadership. I'll show you on the next group we pass. By the way, one week later I found my socks under the windshield wiper on the truck at the spike station. So everything ended up OK for her."

Heading up and out of the Post Corral Creek drainage, Clyde and Pablo started the descent to exit the wilderness and get to the trailhead. This was located just after the Hobler Lake turnoff at the top of the grade.

"Hobler Lake is just about a twenty-minute walk," Clyde said. "Nice place for large groups that don't want to hike too far their first day. Named after a guy named Sig Hobler. Cattleman in these parts in the 1800s. Pablo, here comes a hiker now. Ask where he's going."

The hiker was a lean, fit guy in his early forties carrying a light pack and taking big strides. Clearly he was a chest pounder, one who brags about how many miles he can hike in a day. The downside is chest pounders usually only see ten feet in front of them and miss most of the scenery.

Pablo slowed Jay down, then came to a stop while the lead hiker politely stepped off the trail. "Gettin' a late-afternoon start today I see," Pablo commented with a pleasant smile.

"Yeah, some of these kids in the group I'm leading couldn't get their act together," he said. "Wouldn't get up until past nine o'clock. Farted around until well past noon before we got started. These teenagers don't have a clue once they get off of their couches and away from TV and Xboxes. Going to be a long week for me."

"Where ya headed for today?" Pablo asked nonchalantly.

"Hobler Lake. How much farther is it anyway?" the leader asked, scratching his chin.

"Not too far. The turnoff is at the top of this grade. Relatively flat after that all the way to the lake. Should make it easy before dark. How many are in your group anyway?" Pablo looked down the trail and saw only a couple of backpackers.

"Fourteen," the leader answered without looking back.

"Well, have a nice trip and thanks for stepping off the trail and letting the string by." Pablo made a slight salute and nudged Jay to start walking. The packhorse string was more than ready to get going and finish the day.

After some distance, Clyde said from the tail end, "That was a good question to ask how many are in the group. Let's do a head count on the way out. Might prove interesting."

Sure enough, they didn't see the next hikers until after several turns in the trail. A group of four.

"Where ya headed?" Pablo asked.

"Hobler Lake," the first in the group said with a determined expression.

"You're headed in the right direction. Have a good time," Pablo said politely.

They came across several small groupings along the route, then nothing. "Only counted twelve so far. Been a long time since we saw the last of 'em," Pablo said after turning in the saddle with a concerned look on his face.

"Yep, look up ahead. I see a couple of hikers sitting on that log to the left of the trail," Clyde said, pointing forward.

Pablo rode up alongside, then stopped, and asked, "Where ya headed?"

"Don't know," answered the only one able to lift his head to respond. "Up the trail to some lake. Can't remember the name."

"You with that group up the trail, headed to Hobler Lake?" Pablo asked.

"Yeah, that's it," the leader of the small group said. The other one still couldn't get his head up. Clearly he was exhausted and in misery.

"It's gettin' late afternoon, and you'll have a lot of trouble making it before dark," Pablo said. "You might want to camp right over there by the creek. Last water from here on, or you can come with us back to the station and try again in the morning."

"Nah, we best keep going," the spokesman said. "Group leader called us a bunch of pussies this morning. Would prove him right if we gave up here."

"Well, at least fill up all your water bottles before ya head up that grade," Pablo said calmly. "May need it if ya have to bivouac out for the night." The two nodded.

As they continued their final run to the spike station, Clyde said, "Poor leadership is pushing those stragglers to make poor decisions. See the difference between him and Kenja? By the way, you're catching on fast with the education on wilderness travel. Make your point, but do it with calmness and respect."

Unsaddling and loading in the gooseneck trailer took no time. All seven head were ready to go in fifteen minutes. While traveling the six miles back to headquarters, Clyde and Pablo noticed the beautiful red hue on the granite peaks from the setting sun. End of a good day in the high country.

"Tomorrow, we're headed to Woodchuck Lake. Deb's going with us, since we have five riders," Clyde said with a relaxed smile.

CHAPTER 2

Woodchuck Country

"Wake up, Pablo. It's 5:00 a.m. and the sun beat ya again," Clyde hollered after sticking his head in the opened door. "Time's a wastin'."

Pablo rose slowly, seeing that it was going to be a nice weather day again, judging from the trees and light outside the window. Getting in shape riding all day was a work in progress. Even though he had been riding since a young boy in Mexico, being on a horse all day, every day was taking some getting used to. No problem, though. Clyde didn't push hard, just steady.

With a cup of cowboy coffee in hand, Pablo met Clyde returning down the stairs from Deb's morning bedside coffee delivery. Both walked out to the corral.

"What's going on today?" Pablo asked, looking over the herd. All the horses from yesterday were heads up and ready to go.

"Well, today we have two small groups going to the same place, Woodchuck Lake. Woodchuck is a very large lake, and if we put 'em on each end, they won't much notice each other. Besides, it's a busy lake with other hikers passing through. One group is three people, father and two sons. Father's name is Earl. Earl is about fiftyish, and his sons are about half that. First time for them.

"The other is a group of two. Leader is Bob Carr along with his longtime friend Bill Spangler. They've been coming up here for over thirty years, sometimes twice each year. Both in their early seventies. Those two guys love to fish. Seems that's what they live for. They are around, or on, the lake from dawn till dark. They bring minimal equipment and keep a small camp. No campfire. Say it takes too much attention and would rather fish. Interesting thing is, they never eat what they catch. Always turn 'em back. Stay out usually five days at a time.

"The father and his sons are a different story. Last night, when they came in, I got a look at the gear they wanted to bring in. They say they've been camping many times before, but I'm sure it was with a Mack truck. The ice chest they had took all three to carry out of their pickup. Was at least five feet long and weighed over a hundred and twenty pounds. Told 'em that would never do and gave them three bear-resistant chests to divide the food into. Did that last night, and we'll see how it worked," Clyde said with an exasperated sigh.

After the clients put their gear on the loading dock, located in the center compound, Clyde and Pablo were able to get a clear picture of the magnitude of supplies they had brought. On one side was Carr's load: two small tents, one cooking kit, all their food, sleeping pads, water bottles and such, and one luxury (but a necessity)—a blowup raft with paddles for fishing. The total weight and volume equaled about two-thirds of a load for one packhorse. These guys had their act together.

The next pile was a different story. Gear included cots, a three-burner stove, a tent the size of a small hotel room, two lanterns, three fold-up chairs, three rolled-up sleeping pads (looked big enough to have been taken from their beds at home), and four cardboard boxes of dried food, in addition to the food in the chests, tables, and three huge sleeping bags rated to minus 60. After that, the pile turned into a blur. Looked like they were going for five months, not five days. Pablo could see Clyde wasn't getting in any better mood as the minutes went by.

"OK, Earl, we need to talk," Clyde said. "I know this is your first packhorse trip, and it's very much different from truck camping. First of all, if ya take sleeping pads, then the cots are not necessary. You can get by with one table and one lantern. That chainsaw and bucket of nails are staying here. It's against wilderness rules. Let's consolidate the boxes into the pack bags so we can whittle this down to two bag loads." Clyde whittled on and on until, to Pablo's amazement, he fit all of Earl's necessary gear comfortably on three packhorses.

As Clyde was packing and loading the gear, Pablo and Deb were leading in horses from the corral and saddling up. They would need a total of four packhorses, five client riding horses, and three saddle horses for the guides. Twelve in all. Woodchuck Lake was a one-day trip, meaning they could get in and out in a working day. No need for packhorses for the guides as they would not be out all night.

Out came the packhorses first: Nosebag, Valor, Cinch, and Tobacco. Nosebag was an Appaloosa horse that came with Clyde when he started horse packing. The horse was over thirty by this time. Valor, a darker sorrel mare named after Valor Lake in Black-cap Basin, was in her early twenties. Cinch was a young buckskin mare in training, and Tobacco was a small paint that probably would never make it past a packhorse level.

Pablo started putting on the crossbuck packsaddles. These he knew from his childhood down in Mexico. They had been used here since the Gold Rush. Deb led in the client saddle horses, Cowgirl, Howdy, Lupin, Spice, and Jigger, and tied them to the hitching rail. She then went into the saddle room and brought out a saddle for each and placed it behind the assigned horse. She had selected only the right-size saddle for the horse and rider after looking over the clients.

Pablo had finished with the pack stock and was starting on the saddle horses. Clyde was about finished with the pack loads when Pablo finished the saddle horses. Pablo then walked over and helped load the pack bags onto the truck bed. While Clyde went into the saddle room to get the tarps and ropes, Pablo went to help Deb with their personal riding horses: Little Shot for Deb, Trapper for Clyde, and Chowchilla for Pablo. None of the horses were used the day before and thus were fresh. No need to "overuse animals when ya don't have to," as Clyde would always say.

When all was ready, they started loading the saddled horses into the stock trailers. Needed two trailers for today, as each could hold only a maximum of ten head.

It was 7:00 a.m. and they were ready to go out the gate. Bob and Bill had been ready for the last half hour but were enjoying the extra cups of coffee. Earl and sons were still putting on socks and boots and brushing their teeth. Clyde elbowed Pablo, gesturing toward Earl's oldest son. He could clearly see he was wearing a toupee, crocked and tilting to the left. "Don't know what's the point, wearing a toupee in the wilderness."

"Qué es toupee? Yo no sé."

"It's a hair hat. A regular hat would serve the same purpose and keep the sun off your face at the same time. However, Pablo, if everybody was the same, this world would be a boring place," Clyde commented with a grin.

Breakfast today was burritos made ahead to save time, and off they went. Dinkey, again, jumped in the truck bed and Patsy lay contently on the porch. Seems she knows the routine and is fine with it. The haul to Woodchuck trailhead was much shorter than up to Courtright. Clyde was in front, then Deb, followed by the clients. Going into the spike station, locking the gate, parking, and unloading the horses went smoothly. Pablo and Clyde started loading the packhorses while Deb fitted the clients to their saddles. This required setting the stirrup lengths to each rider just so they could barely stand up in the saddle. Deb had to set the cinch by pulling tight on the latigo strap to make sure the saddle wouldn't move. Clyde always said, "A slipped saddle is the most common reason people get hurt on horses."

With everyone about ready to mount up and ride, Deb called out, "OK, gentlemen, I need all of you over here for a moment. Let's go over getting on the horse first. With the left foot in the left stirrup you hop up. Don't hoist yourself by the saddle horn. This only pulls over the saddle and things get ugly fast."

Bob and Bill had seen this drill many times but patiently observed and waited. Mr. Toupee was busy grooming himself, which Deb quietly noticed, as did Bob and Bill.

"I need everyone to pay attention," Deb continued. "When you dismount, the safest way is to remove your left foot from the stirrup, lean slightly forward, remove your right foot from the stirrup, and swing it around behind you. You will end up lying across the saddle on your stomach. You can then push off the saddle and drop to the ground away from the horse's feet. If ya slide off, you'll end up under the horse and get stepped on. This way, too, your left foot is already out of the stirrup and won't get hung up. Getting off like in the movies can leave your left foot attached to the saddle, and if the horse spooks, you could get dragged. That would definitely wreck your day. Next time you're watching a horse race on TV, you'll notice the jockeys doing the same thing.

"When riding, all the horses are trained to neck rein. That means just rotate both reins to the left and the horse's head will turn in that direction, and with a little nudge with your heels the rest of the horse will follow. The same for turning right. To stop, only give a gentle and short pull on the reins. To continue pulling tells the horse to back up. All horses have a blind spot behind them and they could stumble. To go forward, relax on the reins and give a gentle heel kick. Everybody got that? Perfect, now we're all experts.

"We need everyone to stay together, no dropping back. If you do, the horse will have to run and catch up. That's not an option here. Keep to a walk at all times. Trotting or running is hard on the horses, wears 'em out fast, and is dangerous for you. That's usually when people fall off. If your horse stumbles or scrambles over some rocks, don't panic and jump off. Remember, the rocks are not soft. The last thing your horse wants to do is fall down. Trust your animal, stay centered in the saddle, and ride it out. Much safer that way. Don't let your horse graze along the way. They've been eating all night. This morning all were standing around, bellies full, burping and talking politics. Often they will want to stop and get a bite of some particularly green grass. Don't let them. It's only an impulse. It's like going by a Dairy Queen; even though you're full, ya just can't resist.

"Now, another concern is meat bees. They are not really bees but a type of wasp. The big difference is they will continue to bite, over and over, after they land on the horse. Most of the time ya never actually see them. If your horse starts acting up, meaning tossing and shaking its head, stomping its feet and getting agitated, most likely we're into a wasp area. We need to vacate up the trail fast. So, if that happens, holler out 'Beeees!' That's the signal for all in front to kick their horses and move out fast up the trail. We need to travel only about thirty yards and all will return to calm. Don't panic and do the natural reflex of pulling back on the reins. That is the exact opposite thing of what you should do and is extremely dangerous. To do that is to tell your horse, let's stop here in the beehive so you can continue to get bit. Sorry, the horse has a different idea, and his response will be, let's buck you off so I can get outa here.

"OK, so if your horse wants to drink from any stream we cross, let 'em. Our motto is they can have all the water they want. Keeping hydrated is extremely important up here. When they have spent their lives being able to drink whenever they want, they know there is no need to overdrink. Also, if ya need to take your jacket off, get a drink out of your saddlebag, or have an urge to pee, just holler 'Hold up.' Don't use the word *pee*. It sounds too much like *bee*. Any questions? OK, we're ready to go. Don't worry, we'll start out slow and stay that way. So, follow me."

Deb set out first, leading all five riders. As the last client went out of view around the corner, Clyde said, "Pablo, Deb has the hardest job in the outfit. She has to keep an eye on each one to make sure they stay tight, in line, not pass, not lag behind, sit up straight in the saddle, don't yank on the reins or try to whip their horse. All this while she's a woman in a man's world. She gets this done while they happily comply. They get the idea she is genuinely there for their safety and the clients respect her for it. How she pulls it off I'll never know."

"Maybe that .357 on her hip has something to do with it," Pablo commented quietly.

"Maybe you're right. Anyway, Pablo, the women are taking over this world and will probably do a better job. It's hard for us guys to accept, but in the end, I think we'll be grateful, or at least should be. The other reason we generally follow behind is those darn meat bees. A trait I have noticed is that they generally do not bother the lead riders but are stirred up when they pass by and usually attack the horses toward the back of the string. I would rather have them bite the packhorses in back where I have control than have a client get out of control."

Pablo and Clyde made their way up to trail and soon caught up with Deb and the clients. The wilderness boundary was a good place to stop and check cinches. Pablo was always amazed at how much they loosened up after only a short while. The horses always stood still and in line during this process. The clients seldom ever had to get off the horse.

Soon they were on their way again, dropping down to the Woodchuck Creek crossing. The creek looked like no big deal, but the bottom was full of large, round, and slippery rocks. The horses often scrambled to get across.

"Let the horses go across at their own speed," Clyde hollered. "Only give gentle nudges. Simply hold on to the saddle horn and let the horse do its job. They may scramble, but the last thing they want to do is fall down. Best to just stay in the saddle and ride it out. You'll tend to live longer that way."

All got across fine and off they went up the other side. Going back and forth on the switchbacks, they could see many different

Jeffrey Pine

types of trees. In addition to the Jeffrey pines, there were yellow ponderosa pines, sugar pines, and even a few black oak trees.

"Quite a mix of trees in this area," Clyde explained. "You see the ponderosa pines with their irregular branches going up all sides to the top. Over here is a sugar pine. Notice the long pine cones on the ground at its base. Some are almost two feet long. See the small black oak on the right and a larger one farther over. They are generally a lowland tree, but some of these survive here. Because of all these types of trees and a few extremely large ones, some botanists

Sugar Pine

would call this a flowerpot area. You'll see these often if you slow down and just look around. Many times, people are in a hurry to simply get to their destination. They blow through these areas and never notice the beauty."

As they continued up the canyon, Clyde called up, "Pablo, see that peak high on the left. That's the opposite side of Loper Peak. Over to the left is a place called Cape Horn. I hear it was named by the US Geological Survey team. Guess they thought it reminded them of Cape Horn in South America."

Up the trail they soon came upon a trail turnoff with a sign indicating Chimney Lake to the left. Clyde called out, "I understand that was named in 1945 by a Mr. Rae Crabtree, a prior owner of my station. Says he saw a rock monument looking like a chimney. I guess he was scrounging for names same as me. On up farther we'll be able to look down and see Indian Spring Meadow. Named after an artesian spring coming straight up out of the meadow. Best water you'll ever have. I hear the Indians spent a lot of time there. They clearly knew a good thing when they found it. Would be real easy to just walk past if ya weren't paying attention."

As they headed up toward the top of Crown Pass, the views became drop-dead gorgeous. Not only could they see over the tip of the crest of the Sierra Nevada, but they could turn in the saddle, look west across the California Central Valley floor, and see the Coast Ranges. Pablo thought he could see at least a hundred miles. Woodchuck Lake soon came into view. This level of beauty Pablo had never encountered before. Perched on top of the world was the most beautiful deep-blue lake he'd ever seen. It was surrounded by mostly granite and some Western white and lodgepole pines. Not another soul was in sight.

Bob Carr and Bill Spangler unloaded at this end of the lake. Then Deb continued around to the opposite side with Earl and sons. Unloading Bob and Bill took, at most, ten minutes. They couldn't wait to get their raft in the water and start fishing.

"It's amazing how energetic these two old guys are," Pablo commented. "They've been in the saddle for the past four hours and never complained. Now, look at how they are jumping around like schoolkids on an Easter egg hunt."

"Yeah," Clyde responded, "that's the difference between biological age and chronological age. That's where use-it-or-lose-it comes in. You see the body will respond well to continued steady use. Helps to keep muscles and bones in good tone longer. If ya sit most of the time, time catches up much faster. That's why I never plan on retiring and doing nothing. It's like saying you're ready to lie down and quit. If you do retire from a job, go find another one and keep busy. Even if it involves a whole new career. Older people need to just keep pushing forward. Always have to remember, you're allowed many lives in this world but allowed to die only once."

As Pablo and Clyde trailed around the lake to join Deb with Earl and sons, Pablo was in awe of the view looking west over the lake surface and beyond. It was the image of an infinity pool, followed by the Coast Range Mountains, over a hundred miles away. Clyde, following along behind, could read his mind. "Yep, never get tired of that sight. Even though it's a rough ride or walk up here, this picture should be shared by all. Putting this image on everyone's computer screen saver would be a wonderful thing. All may not be able to get up here, but just knowing it's here is a tranquil and soul-settling experience. That's why having designated Wilderness Areas is a benefit for all."

At the north-side camping location, the clients were already off their horses, and Deb was busy taking off the bridles and tying up stirrups. This measure prevents the empty bridles and stirrups from getting caught on branches on the way down.

Earl and sons were laid out flat like beached whales. All were groaning about aches and pains. Pablo thought Mr. Toupee was about to call out for his mother. As Clyde and Pablo started untying lash ropes and pulling off top tarps, Earl and sons started to show signs of life, rolling over on all fours. Off came the first load, then the last two shortly after. Their gear piling up in front of them, Earl and sons decided things weren't going to get better by themselves. Staggering to get upright, one at a time, they stumbled over to their pile of gear and began to set up camp.

Pablo felt sorry for them. He looked at Clyde and quietly asked, "Should I go over and help, at least to get their tent up and all?"

"Nope, this is what I call their wilderness experience. Along with the beauty, there's also the work. Don't want 'em to feel cheated," Clyde said.

"Start folding the top tarps and coil up the ropes. We can double the empty pack bags inside each other, then put the tarps and ropes inside. That way we can cut our horse loads in half. Faster that way. Remember, older horses go out empty. They've earned it. I'll go string the empty saddle horses together."

Tying the empty saddle horses together was done by taking the number two horse's lead rope and running it up the left side of the number one horse. Go around the neck and tie a bowline knot. Leave a large loop so as not to choke them if the animals behind pull back. Then, take the loose lead line and secure it to the tail of the front horse. Angle the tail forward. The tail is about one-half the bowline knot. In this manner, the tail keeps the lead rope from dropping down and getting between the front horses' rear legs. The hair part of the tail is the only portion in the knot. Never is the tail pulled on, though, since the tension is at the neck. That's the reason for angling the tail forward to allow for this if the rear horse pulls back. All five were tied together, and the packhorses were ready to go in no more than twenty minutes.

"Let's go say our good-byes to the group and head out," Clyde said. He and Pablo walked over to Earl and sons. Clyde told them, "Enjoy yourselves, stay safe, keep the food in those bear containers, and we'll see ya five days from now around noon, since we have to ride up here in the a.m. Be packed and ready to load up. If ya feel like day hiking, there is a nice lake over the pass to the east called Crown Lake, and you can also go over the hill to the west and see Chimney Lake. Ya saw the turnoff on our way up. Good luck on the fishing and have fun, guys."

"On the ride out, Pablo, you lead with the pack string, Deb can follow up behind, and I'll be behind her with the five empty saddle horses. No offense, Pablo, but given the choice, I'd much rather look a Deb's backside all the way out than yours."

It was time then to have lunch. This is customarily called a sit-down lunch. That means eating while sitting on the saddle. Keep traveling is the motto. After about an hour, heading down a different route just to make a loop, they soon came upon a meadow the trail bordered.

Clyde called up to Pablo, "This is Moore Boys Meadow. Named after the Moore brothers who had the cattle permit here. Been long gone, though. Still evidence of the last of the logs for their cabins over to the right. Almost finished melting back to nature. I guess the last generation wasn't too interested in the cattle business. I hear they just let it go back to the US Forest Service. Turns out, I own most of their original ranch down in the foothills. We live there in the off-season with all the horses and cattle. Take everything down in the fall—horses, cattle, dogs, and even Deb here. She says that only happens if I'm nice to her. Says I have to be on good behavior all the time. Tells me I'm on the bubble every day. Can you believe that, Pablo, me being so darn good-looking and all?"

Pablo knew Clyde was starting one of his routine antics, especially when Deb was around. Turning around in the saddle, he noticed Deb was rolling her eyes and shaking her head. He knew what she was thinking. "I give up. He's hopeless."

A short time later Clyde started in again. "Pablo, the name of that horse you're riding is Chowchilla. Got 'im from a guy who lived in that town just up the highway north of Fresno. Never could remember the name he gave 'im so I just named the horse after the town he came from. Deb is riding Little Shot. Named after a lake over in Red Mountain Basin. Short little paint. She likes 'im even if her long legs hit every rock and log we pass on the trail. I'm riding Jigger. Named after another small lake in Red Mountain Basin. Both these horses have the same mother. Named Courtright. You got it, so I can keep track of the lineage.

"Right up ahead on the left and continuing across the trail and down to the right are the remains of the old natural log drift fence. Used to keep the cattle from heading down out of Moore Boys Meadow. They would hold 'em there until all were gathered, then head down in one big drive. Not much left of the fence. It, too, will soon totally disappear.

"On ahead we'll come to a steep and rocky set of switchbacks. Back in the early '80s, I came upon a private horse group there. One of the guys in the group had just gotten a hot-blooded thorough-bred horse. Wanted to bring it up here and try 'im out. Well, when he got to this rough, rocky part, the horse didn't know what to do. Instead of getting off and walking the horse up slowly, he stayed on and kept kicking with his spurs and whipping his neck and butt. Finally, the horse bolts up the trail. Didn't make it, though; broke his leg. The guy had to carry all his gear and saddle back out of the forest himself. Served him right. On top of that, later I heard, the horse cost the guy $7,000, and he had only paid the first $500. Still owed the balance. Never knew how it turned out. If it was up to me, I'd've been using the spurs and whip on the guy all the way out.

"Nosebag's the name of the horse behind you," Clyde contin-ued. "Had him before I got the station. Can put any load on 'im and go all day. Even was forced to overload a few times and he never complained. Used to be a saddle horse, but after a few years he would suddenly start bucking for no apparent reason. Kept this up and it got old fast. I call that being counterfeit. Can't trust 'im. Guess it's his way of saying forget this carrying you around all day. I'd rather pack loads. That way I'm only loaded half the day and empty the other half. Maybe he's smarter than I give 'im credit for.

"Hey, right up here you'll see a four-foot-diameter log across the trail. Deb and I were coming out this trail several years back during a big-time rainstorm, high wind and lightning. She was about fifteen minutes ahead of me with the empty saddle horses. Went through here fine. When I came up, this huge tree was down across the trail. Her tracks led up to and under the tree. I stopped, scratched my head, and slowly approached, calling quietly, 'Deb, are you OK?' No response, though. Then seeing her tracks continue out the other side, I determined she made it. Figured that out all by myself. Had to go through a bunch of brush and crap to get around the new fall and catch up. As you can see, the Forest Service has since cut the log section out of the trail."

Finally, the departure spike station came into view. After pulling up and stopping at the hitching rails, the horses stood still, knowing the routine. Even Dinkey knew her place, patiently waiting until the last horse was loaded before hopping into the back of the flatbed.

"Clyde, do you want me to ride with Deb back to keep her company?" Pablo asked.

"Go ahead and ask, but I'll bet she's had enough testosterone for one day. See what she says."

Returning in less than a minute, Pablo said, "You were right. She said stay with the old man; he'll probably need the help. Guess that's her polite way of saying quiet time sounds better."

"You're catching on. By the end of the summer, you might be closer to figuring out how women think. Good luck with that.

"Look way across Wishon Lake as we're going over the dam. That opening in the mountain is the road to the underground power station. Ya see, PG&E pumps this water up to Courtright Lake at night by reversing the turbines. Then during the day and peak need hours, they let it travel back down the same tunnel and through the turbines again only in reverse to make electricity. Then the next night the same thing is repeated.

"Looking out over the mountains, you'd never know there was a huge power plant under 'em. The plant has three huge turbines. The room is three stories high and as big as a football field. Reusing the same water over and over, smart! The facility is called the Helms Pumped Storage Plant. Named after William Helms. He was friends and partners with a fella named Frank Dusy. They both were sheepmen in the 1860s and '70s. Incidentally, Frank Dusy had a dog named Dinkey. Over by what now is called Dinkey Creek, Frank came upon a grizzly bear that wasn't in the mood to share the trail. The bear attacked Frank. His small dog, Dinkey, jumped in tearing after the bear. That was enough to change the bear's mind and Frank escaped. Dinkey got the worst of it. Was so torn up he died. Frank named the creek where it happened after his dog. Always wanted a dog named Dinkey. Now I have one."

After they pulled into headquarters, Clyde and Pablo unloaded the horses, which took only minutes. The horses thoroughly enjoyed being unsaddled and turned out into the corral to roll in the dirt and eat. While Deb was in cooking dinner, Clyde and Pablo fed the horses. Each grabbed a bale with the hay hooks, dragged the bales out on the wide catwalk, and cut the hay twine, separating the bales into flakes and tossing them into the large feed bins. There was always plenty of hay left from the morning feed-out. However, it was best to leave plenty for the horses that stayed behind that day to eat. That way, the tired and hungry horses that came in didn't have to fight the rested ones. They were full and not motivated to challenge. Things stayed peaceful that way.

Being full from dinner and with tired muscles, Pablo went to bed early, knowing the next day would bring new challenges and adventures.

CHAPTER 3

Pissers

"Wake up, Pablo. Better hurry or the sun's gonna catch you without your boots on again," Clyde hollered from outside the bunkhouse door.

After about ten minutes, both were walking out to the corral, cups of cowboy coffee in hand. Pablo noticed that Deb always took her time getting up, savoring to the last drop the coffee delivered to her bedside.

"We got an interesting group going in today. Family of brothers who grew up back East and relocated here in California while in their twenties. In their fifties now, but you would never know it. Not in a good way. Seems they've been hitting the booze since they were weaned off their mother. The eldest brother, Robert, is the leader. An accountant from down south who definitely likes hitting the bar scene. Showed up here last night with a barfly he picked up while on the way here. I met her last night for just a moment, but that was enough for me. I thought about mentioning if he asked his wife first but just walked away instead.

"Anyway, I heard a bunch of fussing way after dark, and finally a car pulls out and takes off. Turns out Robert took his princess back down the hill, dumped her off in a hotel room, and came back up. He and all the others were up all night drinking. Nobody is stirring over there yet, but don't worry, I'll take care of that shortly.

"Deb's going in with us today. She's best with the riders, but this group is definitely not one of her favorites. Every year is the same. Most of 'em show up early and are soused when they get here. They'll be hitting the hooch first thing but will try to hide it from me, since they know I don't allow drinking and riding. Makes for a dangerous situation. All the brothers look forward to this once-a-year trip. The other fifty-one weeks of the year they spend in front of their TVs watching old Western movies, over and over.

"See that odd trailer over there, with the saddles strapped on the two hitching rails going from front to back. Guess they make their own saddles and want all to see during the trip up here from LA. I let 'em use their own on my horses only because the ride is so short.

"Yeah, the most they can stay on the trail is two hours. That's after stopping every twenty minutes to pee. No surprise where Deb and I got the name for this group; we call 'em the Pissers. They also think after all that hard work with the remote, they're experts on being a cowboy. A couple of years ago, one of the brothers was insisting on wearing his spurs while he rode. After advising him about the dangers and that neither Deb nor I use them, he was still insistent. I finally shrugged my shoulders and said, 'Fine with me.' He immediately displayed a triumphant smile. I followed up with, 'OK with me while you're walking in. Have fun.' That ended the conversation. His spurs were removed before he even got close to my horses.

"Pablo," Clyde continued, "there's six of them, and with the three of us, we'll need nine saddle horses. No need to do any saddling for the six, but we'll have to bring saddle blankets and bridles. This group never remembers those. So, get out Cowgirl, Trapper, Lupin, Cloud, Howdy, and Spice. How about you getting Jigger for yourself, Little Shot for Deb, and I'll ride Valor today. We'll need five packhorses, so let's pull out Pearl, Loper, Nevada, Nosebag and Diamond X."

After all were led out of the corral and tied to the hitching rail, Clyde said, "Go ahead and start saddling up. I'll go wake the darlings and have 'em get their gear on the loading dock so we can prepack."

As Clyde approached the camp, he could hear them stirring inside, obviously passing a flask. He didn't open the tent door flap, just hollered at the top of his voice, "Time to rise and shine, ladies. Need your gear on the dock in fifteen minutes. Gonna pull out in forty-five."

Walking away. Clyde could hear muffled groans. Smiling, he could visualize their heads pulsating.

In an hour, everything was loaded up. Both trailers had seven horses each, and the group's gear in the back. Both Dinkey and Pasty hopped in and headed out the gate with the clients following. The haul over to today's trailhead took only fifteen minutes. Going by the Wishon store, Clyde was relieved to see it hadn't opened yet, because he knew the group would want to stop and get more beer.

The load-up at the trailhead took much longer than usual, Pablo noticed. Deb took charge supervising the saddling. Different saddles could only go on certain horses owing to the shape of their backs. This didn't sit well with a couple of the brothers. One of them said, "I want that paint horse named Howdy over there and my saddle is going on 'im." Well, a direct order to a lady with a .357 on her hip doesn't go very far, Pablo noticed.

Deb replied politely with a slight cutting edge, "Your saddle is too small and will only hurt the withers of my horse. That saddle of yours can only go on Cloud over there. He's a narrow Arabian and won't get sore by your narrow fork saddle frame. Or if you insist on riding Howdy, you will have to put that saddle away and use one of ours. The choice is yours."

Pablo noticed no further conversation. The brother promptly picked up his saddle and walked over to introduce himself to Cloud. Soon different declarations of despair could be heard. "Clyde, do you have a cinch I can borrow?" Another chimed in with "Yeah, I guess I need one of those straps to tie the saddle with. Didn't see it was missing when I put it on the trailer from home." Clyde rolled his eyes and reached inside the gear bag he always brought with extra parts such as cinches, latigos, stirrups, bridles, and so on. Pablo could see why Clyde always frowned when people wanted to bring their own riding gear.

After all the horses were saddled and the clients were on their mounts, Deb went through the usual orientation of horse handling. Pablo noticed few of the clients were paying serious attention, most looking as though they were already experts and didn't need the talk. Deb observed this too and deliberately slowed down the routine so the clients could do nothing but listen. Soon, all were headed up the trail, Deb in the lead. She knew if she allowed any one of them to ride in the front, they would soon be kicking their horses and running up the trail. If that ever happened, Pablo just knew he would hear a loud bang from Deb's gun. Yep, safer for all to have Deb lead.

"OK, Pablo, let's finish packing these loads and get caught up with Deb before she shoots too many of 'em. Ya see, she has the toughest job, putting up with a bunch of boisterous, chest-pounding, hungover guys who are feeling liberated being away from their wives. Remember, her gun holds six shells, and the real scary part is she can reload fast. Let's hurry; maybe we can still save some of 'em."

After about twenty minutes, Pablo and Clyde were able to catch up with Deb—easy, since the brothers were already on their first pee stop. The outfit was on its way to the Chain Lakes, a nice group of three lakes that have a lousy reputation for fishing. The brothers didn't care, since there wasn't a fishing pole in any load. All they wanted was a place to be alone and holler all day and night.

As they rode on, Clyde called out to Pablo and the clients, "That rock outcropping high on the left is Finger Rock. Top is about 9,600 feet. Named during the 1908 US Geological Survey trip. It's a great reference point, since you can see it from parts of Blackcap, Bench Valley, and Woodchuck Lake. Soon we will be crossing a small creek, after which we will turn right and head up to the Chain Lakes."

Soon they did cross the creek and Pablo noticed the trail sign indicating the Chain Lakes to the right but also Duck Lake to the

Sign for Rancheria Trailhead and Duck Lake

left. Pablo turned in the saddle, pointed, and asked what that lake was like.

"It's a small lake, about three acres," Clyde said. "Hear it was named back in the 1940s, again by my predecessor, Rae Crabtree. Gave it that name simply 'cause he saw a duck on it. Guess he too was getting short on names.

"Several years ago Deb and I took somewhat of a California television legend named Huell Howser up there to Duck Lake. He's a guy that went all over doing TV broadcasts about things of interest in this state. Called the show *California Gold*.

"Anyway, we packed in him, his production manager, cameraman, and the California Fish and Wildlife fishery boss, Dale Mitchell. There were doing a story called 'Trout,' about stocking fish in these high-mountain lakes by airdrop. Mr. Howser went to see the fish hatchery in the morning, then got on a plane and made several dive-bomb runs of high Sierra lakes. I hear he got sick big time, but I never saw that on the show.

"Incidentally, Deb and I had been up in the same plane several years prior. A whole lot of fun sitting up behind the pilot, coming in just twenty feet above the granite cliffs, then nosing straight down toward the lake surface. All you see through the front windshield is water rushing up at you fast and hear the engines revved to red-line. The rpm was needed for the climb out. When we're about 150 feet above the lake, the pilot pulls up and opens the bomb bay doors and out go from one to three thousand fingerling trout. Mostly finger-length rainbows. He would then bank to the right or left, and ya could see all the fish hit the lake like throwing out a bucket full of pebbles. We would then scream our way out just over the treetops and head to the next lake drop. Talk about a rush.

"Anyway, I've been told that episode has been re-aired over forty times. Not only here but all over the state. Folks still can't wait to tell me about it whenever it gets rebroadcast. Mr. Howser has passed away, but I think he did these shows for about twenty-six years. He donated his whole estate to higher education. Definitely a guy who left his mark in this world."

After arriving at Upper Chain Lake, they unloaded the brothers' gear. Deb was happy to get the clients off the horses. Only then did she breathe a sigh of relief, knowing all got in without any damage. Pablo observed the lake had its own unique character—rock bound and with a backdrop wall of sheer granite. This is postcard material, he thought.

They lined the string out for the ride home. Pablo took the five packhorses, Deb followed, then Clyde led the empty saddle horse string. Shortly after starting back, Clyde called up to Pablo, "I should tell ya about the time I took a group of rugby players from the coast over to Crown Lake. Ya haven't seen that lake yet, but we'll get there. Anyway, they were heavy boozers too. I packed in fourteen cases of beer for 'em. Never understood why people want to pack in beer anyway. All it is is cans of water, but I guess that's beside the point. Got 'em all in, people, gear, and booze. Not a dent in a single can.

"The next morning, after saying my good-byes, I headed out empty toward home. Along the ride, I did the math. If this group was to drink all that beer, they would have to down one every forty-five minutes each, around the clock. Just thinking about it made my stomach ache and head hurt. Anyway, when I returned, I discovered, they did just that. Every one of those cans was empty, smashed, and piled up. The group had stayed up all night, every night, and never stopped downing 'em. It took one whole packhorse to haul out all the empty, flat cans. I still can't believe it. The group never did come back, though. I found out that within a year, most of 'em were in rehab. No surprise. But to each his own. At least a clean camp was left and the wilderness survived. Can't say the same for them.

"While we're on the subject of impaired people," Clyde continued, "right up here reminds me of the time a search was out for a supposed lost pair of hikers. They came from a group named Pike. I've packed resupply food for them several times in the past. The father was an odd duck. Most of his load was slabs of cured bacon. I couldn't believe how addicted he was to the stuff. When he would open the load and got a good inhale of the aroma, he would immediately just zone out for a good fifteen minutes. Bizarre. When the whole group came up to get the resupply, the same thing happened to them. Thought I was in the *Twilight Zone*. No surprise since they were all bragging about how much weed they were carrying with 'em.

"Anyway, years later I heard about them again, from a SAR team—that's Search and Rescue—organized by the county sheriff's department. Seems two of the group wandered off and couldn't be found. It was right around here. As you can see, we're not that far from the trailhead. Remember, this group has been in these same hills regularly for several years. The search went on for several days before they were finally found, both unharmed. I heard quietly through my sources, these two didn't want to be found. They played hide-and-seek the whole time. Thought it was a great game, putting all those public-paid personnel to work and away from the real job of protecting the law-abiding people down in the flats. I feel the best cure for that type of behavior is cost recovery. Yeah, that's right. Cite 'em and charge 'em. That might make some people think twice.

"Another time, a young lady wanted to go mountain climbing over at the Obelisk. It's a rock dome just inside the park, a little to the south and east of us. Well, she couldn't find anybody to go with her so she just decided to go on her own. She was found several days later strapped to the end of her rope over a rock cornice, dead. The SAR team said she slipped on a rock crevice, got hung up with the rope around her chest, and suffocated. You'll find in this world, Pablo, that some people make very poor decisions. Sometimes it adversely affects others and sometimes it negatively affects themselves big time.

"I should tell you about the time I was traveling in Europe." Pablo could only lower his head, resigned to the fact there was no escaping Clyde's monologues. Deb just rolled her eyes, thinking about how much longer this trip was going to take.

"Well, Pablo, it started out when I was seventeen, about one year younger than you. I worked in the fields out on the west side of central California, along with all the migrant farm laborers. Started out with fifteen of us Anglos from high school. After two weeks of working six days a week, twelve hours a day in 105-degree heat, I was the only gringo left. Lived in the same camps as those migrant workers. Saved a heck of a lot of money 'cause I never had time to spend it.

"Well, I saved enough to go hitchhiking around Europe the following summers. Went there twice for almost three months each. Spent only two dollars a day average. Before I was twenty, I had sixteen foreign country stamps on my passport. Anyway, I was in a place called Istanbul, Turkey. The place was crawling with guys my age there for the wrong reason. Bragged about how much hash they could get for so cheap. All I could think of was how insane that was. I proclaimed they would be better off in the middle of Times Square than here, explaining that Turkey was just looking for American guys to bust just to make examples out of 'em. They only dismissed me, saying I was being an idiot.

"Well, I left in late August to get back to school. One of the guys, who was just a face in the crowd, I later found out was named Billy Hayes. He got caught at the airport trying to bring a bunch of that stuff back here to sell. He spent three years in jail in Turkey before escaping. He went on to have the dubious distinction of being the subject of the movie *Midnight Express*. Thus the point—poor choices, eventually, always lead to poor outcomes. Keep that in mind as you travel down the trail of life.

"Might want to check that second packhorse. Lead rope's getting a little loose. That's it, good. Don't want a wreck if we can avoid it."

After fifteen minutes of riding the peacefulness was broken again by Clyde chiming in. "Hey, Pablo, let me tell ya about another group we took to the same Chain Lake. Well, actually, Deb took 'em in. A bunch of old guys in their mid-eighties. All hikers except one of 'em wanted to ride in. He was the youngest, maybe in his early seventies. However, he was by far in the worst physical condition of the group. Why some people let themselves get so pathetically out of shape is beyond me. He thought a horse ride in would make it simple. Remember, it's only a two-hour ride. Anyway, by the time they get there, Deb had to lift him out of the saddle, he was so stiff. When his feet hit the ground, he could only stand there, holding on to the saddle horn next to the horse. The riding horse was gentle and just stood there, being his support post.

"Some people think horse riding in the wilderness is like a rickshaw ride. Nothing could be further from the truth. This group was to hike themselves out with light backpacks. About five days later, after they hike out, I get a call from this same hiker. Seems he decided on the trail out, about an hour from the end, to just drop his backpack on the trail, hoping someone would come along, pick it up, and haul it out for him. Had the gall to tell me there *might* be fifty bucks in it for them. I told him that the chances of the backpack still sitting there are nil. Who would pick it up and haul it out along with their own backpack. What you are saying makes no sense. His response was, oooh well, guess I'll just leave it. I replied, that would be littering and disrespectful to the wilderness. His response was toooo baaad, and he hung up on me. I waited about a week and rode in myself to look for it, hoping no bear beat me and had it all tore up. I found it, no problem, loaded it up, and hauled it out. Called him to come by the station and get it. He said great, thanks, and claimed he would send a big check for the nonprofit organization I have for scholarship support at CSU Fresno. Well, in the mail came a check for fifty bucks. I promptly wrote a short note back to him, saying this was an insult, he could pick up his gear at the US Forest Service Law Enforcement office, along with his citation for littering. I placed the check with the note and mailed it back to him. Later I heard that coward sent someone else to pick it up for him. But that's OK, because I've never seen him up here since. Some folks have a master-slave mentality and it only makes other people furious. I'm still glad I did what I did.

"Anyway," Clyde continued, "99 percent of the people who come up here are top shelf. They're only interested in a unique wilderness experience. Getting to meet all of them is one reason this occupation is so much fun. A few years ago, I took in two guys. One was an attorney and the other an engineer. The engineer's whole purpose in coming was to fish as many different lakes as possible. The attorney was only interested in photography. Said taking pictures was a lifelong passion. He'd heard about the evening sun on the rocky cliffs toward the back of Red Mountain Basin. So, I packed them to a lake called Devils Punchbowl. It's hugged up against these rock cliffs that are west-facing. Perfect for the setting-sun spectacle. The area has numerous good fishing lakes that were easy to hike to for the engineer. They were delighted with the location, and I waved good-bye and headed out. They were to walk out on their own a week later.

"The next trip I had was with a group to the North Fork of the Kings River, just above the Pot Holes we went by the other day. They were a group of attorneys and doctors, most of whom I already knew. The following day, I took them on a day trip from camp, up to Devils Punchbowl Lake for fishing and lunch. After they were unsaddled and their fishing poles unloaded, all except one took off to fish. The remaining gentleman was a doctor named Mike Adams. He had just retired from a long internal-medicine practice in Fresno and said he was never really much of a fisherman. I suggested we go over to the other side of the lake, explaining I just wanted to check up on the prior group of two. He said sure, admitting the walk would do him good.

"Upon arriving at their camp, I noticed that the engineer had gone fishing and was nowhere in sight, but the attorney came up with a big grin on his face. He explained at length about the wonderful photo ops he'd been getting and couldn't be happier. I did the usual introductions, stating this is Dr. Mike Adams, and the customary handshakes followed. The three of us started walking around the lake, but Dr. Adams said he wanted to take his time to mosey back to the horses, so he set out.

"After Mike was out of sight, I stopped the attorney and said, ya have to promise you won't go ape on me, but I'm gonna let you in of something. Eagerly he complied with a puzzled look on his face. I knew you were obsessed with photography. Well, you just shook hands with Ansel Adams' son. His eyes bugged out and I thought he was going to pee his pants. He claimed Ansel Adams was his idol since childhood but never got to meet him since Ansel had passed away long ago. To his credit, he maintained and stayed cool, never mentioning it to Mike before we departed. I'm sure the engineer got an earful later that evening around camp."

After ten minutes of quiet riding, something Deb was most grateful for, Pablo piped up and asked, "Where did you get Nosebag and how did he get his name anyway?"

"Nosebag," Clyde answered, "came with me when I started out back in 1980. Actually, he was the third horse I ever owned. Remember, I started out as a backpacker. Didn't start riding in this wilderness until after I was out of medical school and in practice.

The only reason I call him Nosebag is that I always wanted a horse by that name. He was another backyard pet that the kids outgrew. The parents called me, and I picked him up for about two hundred bucks. Like I said earlier, he was a saddle horse but then changed his mind. Guess horses can do that same as people.

"Anyway, he's in his mid-thirties and going strong. I've put the most bizarre loads on him and he never flinches. About ten years ago, the California Department of Water Resources needed to be packed into Blackcap Basin. Had to work on that snow pillow I told you about up in Lightning Corral Meadow. They arrived in the early morning with two huge, five-foot-by-five-foot replacement snow pillows for the site up there. There are four of them, but two got damaged and had to be replaced. They were first brought in by helicopter, but you can only do that with snow on the ground. This was August. These pillows are two aluminum panels welded around the edges and have to be filled with nonfreezing fluid. They then are laid flat, and when the snow piles up on them, the pressure pushes the fluid into a sensor that then relays the info to a satellite. Knowing the weight of water, the engineers can determine how much water is being deposited in the Sierra range over the winter. That way they can determine the quantity we will have during the spring runoff. This information is vital to the farmers and to determine any potential for flooding. Early water releases from the dam sites are based on this information.

"Anyway, I had to get these pillows up the nine hour trail to Blackcap Basin. Each weighed a hundred pounds. How to set 'em up on Nosebag's back was the tricky part. I used two old time slings I had. They are canvas tarps and have long leather straps with buckles on one end. After strapping them on, I had to tie the top both front and back together to make the form of a tent on top of the packhorse. That forced the bottoms out so as not to interfere with the animal's legs or feet. Fortunately, each metal pillow had a two-by-four frame holding 'em on all sides. That gave me something to tie to and protected the edges from rocks and trees.

Snow Pillows on Horse

"When all was done, you could only see Nosebag's nose, eyes, and most of his ears in the front. In the back only his tail stuck out. After we loaded everything else, the whole pack string headed up the trail. With Nosebag right behind me, every time that load bumped a log or tree it sounded like hitting a tin roof with a hammer. Nosebag never flinched. Kept on going as if he did it every day before breakfast. Nine hours later, I was delighted to unload those panels first. I thought for sure Nosebag wanted to give me a kiss. I didn't have the heart to tell him then we had to take the two damaged ones back out when we left in three days. Thought I'd save that for later. He ended up taking them out without a single problem.

"You talk about great mountain horses that are worth their weight in gold, Nosebag's one of 'em. Since that horse had a prior owner he probably remembers what that life was like. Being locked up in a small corral for weeks at a time. Getting rode once a month for an hour, then put back in and hearing the corral gate lock shut. Up here, he and all the rest of 'em work four months out of the year, then get eight months off. All done in the high altitude where the air is clean and cool. Gets the best food money can buy and all he can eat of it. Has a lifetime medical and dental plan. Even has a shoe clause in his contract. Yep, Pablo, if you ever want to get reincarnated, coming back as one of my horses isn't a bad choice."

Soon down the trail, the group came upon a family of five. Mom and dad with three stepping-stone children depicting age differences of no more than two years. They politely stepped off the trail to let the horse string pass. Dinkey immediately took up the position, sitting on the boot of the oldest child, hound face staring straight into her eyes, patiently waiting to be petted.

As Deb approached, she stopped next to the youngest girl and asked, "How old are you?"

She replied, "Six years, two months, and eight days counting today."

"Wow," Deb said. "So since you have been carrying that small backpack all this way, I think you deserve the hiker-of-the-day award. Here's a small chocolate bar as your prize for the outstanding effort today."

Deb reached down and handed her the wrapped candy, and the little girl's face lit up with delight. Both parents were impressed with the gesture, declaring Samantha was just about to get real tired and this was the perfect perk-up to motivate her on the last remaining mile to the parking lot. Thank yous were given and off the family went.

After about ten minutes down the trail, when the family could no longer be seen, Clyde called out, "Pablo, I'd be careful about copying that action on the trail by yourself. I call it a classic case of double standard. Deb can give little girls candy all day, but if you or I tried that, we'd probably get arrested. Remember what I mentioned the other day, nobody said life was fair."

Pablo didn't respond, but not because he wasn't contemplating. Yeah, he thought, that would be awkward. Too bad some weirdos have made society so distrusting. A lot of kind actions are not done due to this fear. So seldom do these polite actions happen nowadays that when they do, it makes the evening news as something rare and special. He thought it odd.

Looking up, they all saw the trailhead and both rigs at the same time. Dinkey and Patsy ran up to the trucks and laid down flat on the shady side. Both knew there was no reason to stand around in the hot sun when they could lie down and sleep in the shade. Ranch dogs figure this out fast.

Unloading the pack bags filled with equipment went fast. Each knew the job and pitched in. After they removed the bridles from the guides' saddle horses, they put them in Deb's trailer, one at a time, head to tail, on a slant. With all seven loaded, the gate was shut and she was ready to head out. Clyde and Pablo did the same with the seven remaining horses. They shut the gate and followed Deb down the road to pack station headquarters, the dogs only jumping in at the last second.

Since Pablo was riding shotgun, it was his obligation to open and close the gates. He never minded this chore, for he knew Deb and Clyde probably wouldn't be able to count how many gates they'd opened and closed over the past forty years. The haul back was short, but Pablo never missed the opportunity to turn in the seat and admire the setting sun on granite cliffs and peaks—an image he would never get tired of.

CHAPTER 4

Blackcap

"Wake up, Pablo. Rise and shine. Sun beat ya again. It's already 5:00 a.m.," Clyde hollered from out the window of the bunkhouse.

As Pablo staggered from the cookhouse with the usual cup of cowboy coffee, he once again met Clyde coming down the stairs after his morning ritual of delivering coffee to Deb.

"Where we headed today?" he asked Clyde as they both approached the corral.

"Way up in the back part of Blackcap Basin. To a meadow named Lightning Corral. One of the most beautiful places you'll ever see. A huge, flat, and green meadow with a large and deep creek meandering through from one end to the other. It's about 10,300 feet, almost at tree line. Mostly all granite surrounding the whole thing, with higher lake exit streams cascading down. The horses love it up there and so do I. Can't wait for ya to see for yourself.

"Going to be a long ride, though. About nine hours in the saddle, one way. So we'll have to spend the night and come out tomorrow. We're only hauling gear. Should need about three packhorses for their stuff and another one for our gear. They're all walking. Going to take them two days to get there. That's why they started out yesterday and we'll meet up with 'em this evening. Leader is a guy named Mark Eisele. Has his wife and three daughters. Took off with backpacks and overnight gear yesterday morning.

"Mark has been coming up here every year since I started. He was a young lad then. Just graduated from UC Berkeley. Seen him grow up, get married. Now has the three kids that are almost grown themselves. Two of 'em are in college at Cal Poly over in San Luis Obispo. On scholarship for cross country. You'll see why when ya meet 'em. I hear the youngest wants to go to UC Santa Barbara. Since those kids were little, dad and mom have been bringing 'em up here. Shorter trips to start, then going farther each year. It's twenty-five miles where we're going, and I bet the young ones have to slow up for dad now. His wife, Kathy, she's a real trouper. Hangs with 'em all just fine. By the way, the ladies are lookers too so don't let your eyeballs pop too far outa yer head. That gets embarrassing."

Pablo wondered if Clyde ever took a breath. Time to get working. All the Eisele gear was in duffels and pre-weighed. Poundage written on duck tape attached to each bag. Much like Outward Bound. Pablo was getting quick to pick up on the program. He returned from the saddle room with six leather-canvas bags and put them on the loading dock. He spread them out so they could get at them easy. Pablo couldn't believe how heavy they were. Each one weighed right at sixty-five pounds.

"Eisele has this figured out," Clyde said. "Packs these duffel bags up to the maximum. Gets the most for his money that way. Small wonder he's a successful banker. He'll be out for two weeks. Brings a whole library of books for the family. Good booze too. Be careful with that bag. We will have to pack it with soft stuff snugged up close inside the pack bags. Don't want anything broken if it's rubbed up next to trees or rocks. We'll put this load on the lead packhorse. Can keep an eye on it better there."

After all six pack bags were stuffed and loaded up into the flatbed, Deb, Clyde, and Pablo took care of their own gear. Deb brought out two small tents, both sleeping bags with pad rolls, food in a bear-proof canister, a small one-burner stove, utensils, and a change of clothes. These items amounted to less than fifty pounds. Clyde then packed the shoeing bag. Usually the heaviest item, it contained about eight extra shoes, four fronts and four rears. The rears were pre-shaped, which makes them much faster to put on. The rest of the bag was filled with pullers, nippers, crimper, hammer, nails, rasp, a rear-leg tie-up rope, and a front foot strap.

"I'll go over all this shoeing stuff later. Always take the shoeing gear when you go out overnight. Don't want any animal to have to go barefooted. These granite rocks will sore 'em up fast if ya do," Clyde said. "Let's go get the horses pulled out and saddled. Deb says break-fast is almost ready."

They led out the four packhorses and tied them to the hitching rail. "Now, we'll go ahead and get the two saddle horses. I'll ride Camp today and you can take Jay again," Clyde directed. Saddling the four packhorses and both riding animals didn't take more than twenty minutes. Clyde then went into the saddle room and returned with six straps, about two feet long, three inches wide with a buckle on one end and holes on the other. In between were two three-inch rings separating the strap into three, almost equal parts. He then buckled one around each of the horses' necks. "I will fill you in on how these work and why later." Almost on cue Deb called out, "Frying the eggs."

After the usual hardy breakfast, both strolled back out to the tied-up horses and started loading them into the stock trailer. Clyde led the first one in and Pablo handed him the remaining five, one at a time. With all loaded, head to tail, the trailer rear gate was shut and they were ready to roll. Pablo was always surprised to look down at his watch and note the hour: 7:00 a.m. It always worked out to this departure time even though Clyde never wore a watch.

As they drove up to the cookhouse, Clyde came to a slow stop. "Load up, Dinkey. Patsy, ya got to stay and watch the fort. Will be out two long days and the trip might be tough on ya."

Again, Pablo was surprised to see Patsy just instantly turn and go back to the porch, as if saying, "No problem, have a nice trip. I'll be fine here, eating all the dinner scraps and not having to share. Yep, you guys go on ahead and don't forget Dinkey."

With lunch burritos in their pockets, out the gate they went, hearing Deb's usual callout, "Be careful."

Partway up the road to Courtright, they came to a portion of the road Clyde called Beaver Slide. Pablo asked, "How did you come up with that name for this straight stretch here."

"Every once in a while, we have a late winter. The snowpack can stay until early to mid-July. Outward Bound sometimes calls me to do a resupply around the first part of June, and this six miles of road is solid snowpack. I would go get a snowmobile from folks over at Huntington Lake, put it in the back of the flatbed, and haul it to the start of the road back near headquarters. Off-load on the snow embankment and load up the resupply duffel bags. Two at a time. I'd head up the snow-covered road to Courtright Lake where we would meet up. Most of the time I'd have to make three round-trips.

"Anyway, you can see this straight stretch also goes down at about a 15-degree angle. Look to your right, it's almost a straight drop-off on the downhill side and no guardrail. Covered with snow, the route is higher on the uphill side and you get pushed to the downside by gravity. That's where the fun begins. Hauling down with a load, you're half sliding and must tweak the throttle to aim the machine slightly uphill. Too much throttle, your back end swings around, and too little, the nose goes over. If you screw it up, you're a goner. They probably wouldn't find me until after the snowmelt. When ya survive, ya howl with delight and you know what the beavers on National Geographic feel like. That's why I gave this here spot that name."

Pablo started to admire the sheer granite cliffs seemingly right off the road. Many SUVs were parked, and people were unloading mountain-climbing gear. Clyde noticed Pablo's fixation and said, "This whole area is real popular with the climbers. Ever since it was written up in their magazines. I'm told there are all sorts of climbing levels right close to the road. Makes it much easier. Usually, most of the work to rock wall climbing is just getting to the climb site with all the heavy gear. I've taken numerous climbing groups into the wilderness, and their gear is the heaviest by far. Wouldn't want to carry it on my back very far. Not by choice anyway."

After they backed into the spike station and unloaded the horses and pack bags, Pablo got out the four top tarps and ropes. It took two people to lift each pack bag. First on the right, then the left side of the packhorses. Clyde put on the tarps and let Pablo practice doing the box hitch. All went smoothly, and they were ready to go in less than thirty minutes.

"Pablo, you take the three packhorses. Lead with Pearl like ya did before and then Loper and Poco. I'll pull Nevada with me. He has our gear, and we'll have less chance of getting our stuff mixed up with theirs. Remember, don't coil the rope in your hand. That's it, good. Now let's go."

Riding up the short distance on the jeep road, Pablo noticed three jeeps coming up behind him. As they got up close to Nevada, Clyde turned in the saddle and raised his hand, palm out, to indicate a stop. The three jeeps complied. Clyde called to Pablo, "At the next opportunity, lead the string off the road and let 'em by. Life's much easier for Nevada if he doesn't have a jeep trying to ram him in the butt. The jeep drivers don't understand that this can create a serious problem. It's ignorance, not stupidity; there's a big difference."

Soon the whole string of horses was off the road, including Clyde's. As the three jeeps went by, Pablo noticed the kids had their noses up against the windows, staring out in awe. The moms were taking pictures. Pablo now knew what an animal in a circus act feels like. Clyde called to Pablo, "Smile and wave," then quietly added, "It'll probably be the highlight of the trip for those kids" as he, too, gave a gentle salute.

Up the trail they went, past Hobler Lake turnoff, down by Long Meadow, and on to Post Corral Creek. Clyde instructed Pablo to turn off early, about a hundred yards before the crossing. Somewhat in the area Deb had found the lost UC Santa Cruz hiker.

"Let 'em stand here for a few minutes. Some might want to pee. Don't want 'em doing that in the creek." Sure enough, after the horses had stopped for no more than two minutes, half of them stretched out and took a long urination. "Pablo, you'll notice they pretty much go one at a time. It's like they wait for each other. Would be nice if they all went at the same time. Be much faster. I guess nobody told them to be in a hurry." Soon, all were done, and Pablo led the string back onto the trail and toward the crossing.

While watering the animals, Clyde chimed in, "I remember the time we took a Sierra Club trip in and they overnighted here. We were just hauling gear and they all walked, much like we're doing now. Come morning, it was raining cats and dogs. The group assembled around the leader all pissed off at the weather and shouting profanities. I've never seen that work but thought they knew something I didn't. I think Jay was with me on that trip. We were to continue with their gear on up and into Red Mountain Basin that day and return empty the next.

"Anyway, the leader said time to head out and group shouted, 'We don't hike in the rain.' The leader then made the mistake of calling 'em a bunch of wimps. That's when the whole group exploded and mutinied against the leader. I couldn't believe it when every hiker put on their day packs and headed back down the trail toward their cars. Jay and I looked at each other, shrugged our shoulders, then loaded up their gear and followed them back out.

"I'm not blaming the Sierra Club as a whole. Most groups are gung-ho, no matter what. Everything has to do with the leadership. The vast majority are good, but some, not so much. That guy made the big mistake of insulting his group. Once ya do that, everyone turns you off. He could have been giving 'em the secret to life, but everybody had tuned him out. Perfect example of losing your audience. Moral is, Pablo, if ya want ta lead, hear yer group out. Never cut 'em short. Looks like the horses have got their fill. Time to move on."

About forty-five minutes down the relatively flat trail to the North Fork of the Kings River, their path meandered through a field of low, shrub-type plants. Very woody and different from any Pablo had seen before. Clyde could see Pablo looking down and commented, "Know what those are? They're blueberries. Come fall these plants will be loaded with small fruit that are mighty tasty. The bears think so too. Coming through here in September or October, I frequently see bears here. Fun to watch, but the horses get snorty and I have to keep 'em moving. No stopping or I could have my own mutiny.

"Pablo, now we're coming upon some large trees. See the first one on the left that's over five feet in diameter. That's a red fir. Look

Red Fir

up farther; on the right is another one. Notice all the different types and sizes of trees here. What does this remind you of?"

"One of those flowerpots you were talking about before."

"You're catchin' on. We're about to top out over this ridge and go on down to the North Fork of the Kings River to a place we call the Pot Holes. Will be obvious as we get closer."

As they descended toward the river, Clyde called up, "Pablo, look straight up ahead at that mountain on the skyline. That's Blackcap, and we're going around the backside of it. At the bottom of the cliff on the left of the peak is Guest Lake. That's in a whole different canyon we'll get to on another trip. By the way, many years ago, Deb and I packed in a fishing group from Italy to the Pot Holes area we're coming up to. The leader was a hotshot fly fisherman, said he was well published back in Italy. Also we had along a local news camera crew who just wanted something for the evening show. Guess it was a slow news day. At that time the cameras were huge and cost about $80,000. Needless to say, I was a little nervous about the load. Packed the camera in and out with horse pads stuffed on all sides. Worried the whole time.

"Anyway, we stopped here for lunch, got out the fly rod, and the Italian starts casting. The film crew loved it and got a lot of footage for their newscast. The hotshot fisherman then gave his fly rod to Deb, and she starts casting out for fish. She's wearing cowboy boots, spurs, pistol on her hip, chaps around her long legs, and with her black, curly, 'fro-type hair under a cowboy hat, that fisherman couldn't stop taking pictures. She was standing on an outcropping of rock over there, casting over glass-smooth water in these pools. Well, about a year later, some friends of ours went to Italy and saw posters of Deb on the walls of the sportfishing shops. They said Deb was famous over there, but nobody knew who she was. Deb never got a cent out of it anyway so, ooooh well."

As the string went up the trail, following the river, they first crossed Fleming Creek, then came upon a log cabin between the trail and the creek.

"That is called the Meadow Brook Cabin," Clyde said. "It's a gauging station. Site to measure water flow down the North Fork of the Kings River. Put here by PG&E. The information beams up to a satellite every day. Sometimes every hour. I haul in supplies here every so often. I remember a Sierra hydrologist named Paul Riggs I'd take in. We would spend the night and all he brought to read were magazines on ocean sailing boats. Strange, since he spent his whole life in the mountains. Shortly after he retired I heard he passed away. Don't know if he ever got on a boat."

After five hours in the saddle, they came upon another log cabin at the base of a long meadow. The North Fork of the Kings River ran through the meadow, which was bordered by steep mountainsides and covered with lodgepole and white fir trees, the scene was drop-dead beautiful to Pablo.

Clyde, seeing the wonder in Pablo's face, said, "This log cabin is one of oldest in these hills. I hear it was initially started here in about 1890 by the family of the same Moore brothers we talked about before. They had the cattle permit up here at the time. This is a perfect example of the first generation working their butt off and putting together something big, then the following generations just floating along, not putting in much effort. Finally, the last generation let this all go back to the Forest Service around 1985. Some of the older maps still show this as private property. Never actually saw any of the Moore brothers here. An old cowboy named Bob Simmons ran all the cattle for them. By the way, my foothill ranch has the Moore name way back on many previous deeds. Strange how things work out."

Continuing east and crossing Fall Creek, Clyde spoke up. "Pablo, look on up ahead. It's the Eisele group. We're gonna beat 'em but not by much."

As Pablo and the horse string came up to the group, the Eiseles stepped off the trail to let them pass and say howdy. The Eiseles told Clyde and Pablo they had spent the prior night at the Pot Holes and described the beautiful sky full of stars. Pablo started to move the string again but not in much of a hurry. He noticed the youngest daughter, about his age, petting Dinkey. The savvy dog had planted her rear end on the girl's left hiking boot and was getting all the petting and attention she was hoping for. Pablo thought the girl looked somewhat Hispanic. He softly said, "Tienes una sonrisa bonita." The young girl looked up with a slight grin, gave him a partial wink from her left eye, and promptly focused her attention back on Dinkey, not interrupting the petting. Clyde noticing this said, "OK, Pablo, time to get moving."

After they were about fifteen minutes up the trail and the hiking group was out of sight, Clyde called up to Pablo, "I see you couldn't resist competing with Dinkey for the attention of that young lady, telling her she had a beautiful smile. No chance with that dog around. But lots of luck to ya anyway."

Pablo didn't dare turn around as Clyde would see his red face. He just kept on riding as if he didn't hear a thing.

After a while, Clyde called out, "Pablo, see that mountain with the black tip? That's Blackcap Mountain you saw earlier. Whole top is a type of volcanic rock, all porous. Hear it was named around 1908 by the US Geological Survey. The peak is a little over 11,500 feet. Now look way to the northeast. In the back you can see the top of Mount Goddard. That was named around 1864 by a survey team. It was first climbed around 1879. That peak is about 13,500 feet high. Imagine, it's 2,000 feet higher than Blackcap Mountain right here. Anyway, that peak was named after George Goddard, who was a surveyor and mapmaker for much of this area. I understand he died around 1906."

After they crossed the Kings River and went north, the terrain changed. Nothing but granite slab rock. Winding their way up, choosing the easiest path for the horse string, Pablo was curious as to how the horses could keep their footing on this glacial polished rock. Pablo hollered back to Clyde, "How do these horses stay upright on this smooth rock? Since they have steel on their hooves, ya'd think they wouldn't be able to stand up, let alone walk up this."

"Well, it's like this," Clyde responded. "These horses know how to position their body weight flat on each foot, sometimes relying only on one or two hooves at a time to get balance and momentum. Also, the steel shoes are scratched up and grip better than you think. Going over this granite all day, every day, is why I need to reshoe 'em every six weeks. We'll need to do just that before we head out in the morning. A couple of 'em are getting thin. I'll show you an easy method that you can get started learning and then do the next one. I learned several tricks about shoeing from a cowboy named Jim Hamilton. I remember taking him up to the top of Blackcap Mountain over there. Got all the way to the top on horseback. Can see over twenty named lakes from that perch. He told me it was the most awesome sight he had ever seen."

Finally, topping out and approaching Lightning Corral Meadow, Pablo pulled on his reins and stopped the whole string. Clyde didn't say a word, knowing what was going through his mind. Before Pablo was the most beautiful, frying-pan-flat meadow, about eighty acres, he estimated. It had two large streams meandering through, one originating from the back and the other from the left. Both joined just before exiting and cascading down the granite slab rock they had just come up.

Not wanting to interrupt his moment, Clyde simply waited until Pablo was ready. Finally, Pablo turned in the saddle and asked, "Where to?"

"We're going way over to the far side of the meadow to give the Eiseles their solitude. We'll come back here after unloading and set up camp for the night."

Once the group's gear was unloaded and all had returned to the overnight camp, Pablo finally got off the horse for the last time that day, nine hours after starting.

The lead horse kept tied, the pack string stayed in line, not moving. It was obvious to Pablo that they had done this before. He then helped Clyde unload, starting with the last packhorse and unsaddling him before moving on to the next. Clyde instructed

Horse Hobble on Neck

him to place each packhorse's saddle in a line on a flat granite slab, in the same order as the string. That way there was no problem putting the same equipment back on in the morning. Saves time that way, not having to readjust equipment.

As each horse was relieved of its burden, Clyde reached up and removed the strap from around the neck. Starting from the opposite front leg, just above the hoof, Clyde encircled the strap, then ran the end through the distant ring. Bringing the remainder to the near hoof, he placed the end through the second ring, then around the leg just above the hoof, and finally buckled up. He made sure it was just secure enough to stay on but not too tight as to chafe the animal's skin. On every third horse he would place a bell around the neck. Pablo was surprised to see the unloaded horses not getting agitated. They stood still and awaited their turn. He was also surprised the unloaded horses didn't flee. They simply stood, waiting until all the others were done. Not until then did the whole group hop out and start eating.

That's when Clyde spoke up. "Watch how these animals will stay only in the riparian area for about twenty minutes. After that, it's up the mountainside they go. Up there, in the rocks, is the best grass. I call it rock grass, been told it's a form of a sedge. The ends are full of protein. Much better they spend all their time up on the hillside because then there is no impact on the low, flat, and grassy area. Much easier on the land being up in the granite. Also, fewer mosquitoes.

"These mountain-raised horses aren't dumb. Too many people take their private, flatland horses up here and turn 'em out. They mistakenly think if there is grass and water, why would they leave. Well, the horses don't like getting bit any more than you or I. Just pay attention to the animals and they will tell you where they want to be. Watch, in the morning they'll be in the south- or east-facing slope to get the first ray of sunshine. The younger horses learn from the older ones.

"I never camp with the clients. Over the years, I've let the horses choose where to spend the night. That comes by reason, along with trial and error. Many times, in the earlier days, I would wake up and find the horses a quarter of a mile away. Before rushing up and grabbing them, I would first look around and try to determine why they came to that new location. That's where I came up with all these overnight camp spots. Got about thirty-six of 'em after letting the horses choose. By having so many of them, I never overuse any one place. My goal is to finish the summer and nobody would ever be able to tell where the horses overnighted. Minimal impact is the ultimate goal. Also, never tie your horses up overnight. That to me is a cardinal sin. You'll never see me even use a high line. It puts too much impact on one place. My motto is, If the horses aren't working, they're eating. By morning, all have full bellies, and they are rested and simply standing around talking politics, waiting for the workday to start. That's why they stay in such good condition all year long."

It was time to set up camp before the last ray of sunlight went behind the mountain. They set up their two small tents, both with only netting for a roof. The netting would still let the full magnitude of the evening star show be visible. Eating out of cans, heated over a one-burner stove, and washing the food down with cool mountain water, Pablo was surprised how satisfied he was. Keep it simple. No pots or pans to clean and no fire to mess with. Even Dinkey was satisfied after eagerly eating her canned dog food and plopping down under a small white bark pine, sound asleep. About then Clyde said, "Time to hit your tent and get to sleep. Five o'clock comes mighty early."

Trying to get to sleep, Pablo was fascinated by the endless display of stars above him. He called over to Clyde in his nearby tent, "Why are there so many stars up here? I never noticed that before."

"Mainly, no light pollution. Folks who live in cities like having streetlights everywhere. Makes 'em feel safe. But they give up seeing one of God's true wonders. Or, maybe, since we're almost two miles high, could be we're closer to 'em."

Pablo didn't answer, knowing Clyde was messing with him. Finally, Clyde said, "Tell Dinkey good night and get some sleep."

Pablo's first blurred vision of morning was looking straight up the jagged granite peaks, outlined by the morning sun's advancing rays climbing up from behind. Only then could he hear the sound of Clyde stirring around, getting the coffee going. He had already got dressed, fed Dinkey, and was now warming up the premade breakfast burritos Deb had packed. "Sun's gonna beat ya again," Clyde called, after noticing Pablo sticking his head out of the tent flap. "Hey, Dinkey, go lick Pablo's face. Can see he's not fully awake yet. No way he can sleep through that."

After Pablo stumbled out and had a cup of cowboy coffee in his hand, Clyde said, "Where would you think the horses might be?"

Pablo looked around, considered all that he was told the evening before, and said, "Around the corner, up there to the left. That's where I'd be if I was a horse."

"Now you're thinkin'. Good job," Clyde said. "Finish your coffee and put a warmed-up burrito in your pocket. Let's get these lead ropes and start hiking."

Sure enough, the horses were standing contently, right where Pablo thought.

"First, check to see if they all have their hobbles and bells," Clyde said. "Try not to walk directly straight to a horse. That can make 'im nervous. Walk around to the back, on the uphill side of 'im. That way, if they spook for any reason, at least they will be hopping back toward camp.

"Go to your lead packhorse first, put the lead rope on 'im, and let it hang over this branch. No need to tie off hard. Leave the hobble on 'im 'cause that's his parking brake. Then, on to the next. Put on the lead rope first and simply lay the end across your lap as ya squat down to undo the hobbles. Don't want the lead rope coiled around ya, 'cause if the horse jumps you could easily get caught and be in real trouble. After ya undo the hobble, stand up and put it around his neck, then buckle it up loosely. Good, perfect. Now, take 'em over and necktie to the lead packhorse, then tail-tie like I showed ya before. Keep doing that for all of 'em. Put the packhorses in the same order as yesterday. That way we don't have to re-sort later. I'll get our two saddle horses over here."

After getting all the horses back to camp, Clyde said they needed to do some shoeing. Both front feet on Pearl were getting thin at the toe, and Loper's rears were the same.

"Pablo, bring over Pearl first. I'll do one foot, then you can do the other." Clyde lifted the left front hoof and encircled a long strap with a buckle around the leg just above hoof itself, then up around the upper leg, just below the horse's elbow. This way there was no need to stand and hold the hoof. The horse was completely comfortable and stood still. Securing the shoe with six nails was all that was needed. Clyde kept a little longer nail end out of the hoof after trimming the distant end off and putting it in his pant leg cuff. Always said it is best to leave a long crimp on the nail end. Leaving this hook on the end

Shoeing Front Foot Tied Up

of the nail keeps the shoe on much better in these rocks. Always said that six nails are as good as eight if put in correctly. Done. Took about full four minutes. Pablo then did the right foot in a similar manner. He took a little longer, but the result was the same.

"Perfect," Clyde said. "Now let me show ya on the left rear of Loper."

After running a three-quarter-inch soft cotton rope around the neck and tying it off with a loose bowline knot, he ran the rope down the side, around the left rear leg, just above the hoof and back up through the loop around the neck. This done, he gently lifted the rear hoof, up and forward, to the desired level and tied off with a slip knot around the neck portion. The hoof height was not too high, as this would be uncomfortable for the horse. Pablo noticed the animals were totally at ease with this.

Clyde told him, "Ya start 'em out slow, until they get used to it. The whole trick is for them to see they will not get hurt. You can tell when they understand, 'cause they'll start to relax and not fight. This makes it easy to do the shoeing, saves the wear and tear on your back, and is much safer for you. As you can see, there is little chance

Shoeing A & B Rear Foot Tied Up

you can get kicked. If things go south, you can always stop and pull the slip knot and everything returns to normal. After letting things calm down, ya can start again. First thing ya know, they look at you as a true friend, since you are the one that gets 'em out of the odd situation and back to normal. I'll show ya. Watch his eyes and head. See how he follows me when I walk away. Make sure you have all your tools ready when ya start. Otherwise you'll have to walk away to get 'em and the horse feels he's being abandoned and panics. So, outthink 'em. Ya both will live longer."

Pablo did the same on the right rear, after some initial intimidation, and all ended up well. They were soon loaded up and heading back down the trail toward home, with nine hours ahead of them.

CHAPTER 5

Evac

"Wake up, Pablo," Clyde called out from the hitching rail. "The horses are taking bets to see if the sun beats you up this morning. So far, odds are 3–1 the sun wins. Better hurry or the horse losers won't let ya forget it all day."

Pablo was just lifting his head. The right ear was muffled against the pillow, but the left ear could clearly hear Clyde's declaration from thirty yards away. Coming out the bunkhouse door, he noticed Clyde lifting his cup and motioning toward the cook house. This was an implied command to go get some coffee first and get back to help saddle up.

Returning from the cookhouse, Pablo could hear Deb stirring upstairs, realizing she was done with the morning coffee Clyde had brought her and was fixing to come down and start her day. Walking up to the hitching rail, Pablo asked, "Where to today?"

"We're taking the gear for a group of hikers up to Rae Lake. That's up in Red Mountain Basin, close to 10,000 feet. Since they are all walking, all we will need are three packhorses for them and one for our gear. We'll spend the night, probably jump over the hill to Fleming Meadow after that, and come back tomorrow. This is a nice group of six people, three couples, all in their sixties but go-getters. Most folks would take two days to get there, but this group will make it easy in one. They come every year and head to a different location every trip. Since the packhorses will only be carrying backpacks plus a couple of extra food bags, the loading will go fast. I'm having them keep their gear until we get to the trailhead, and you and I will load it all up there. Since it's only about a six-hour ride, we'll take Patsy today and leave Dinkey since she goes on most of the long trips. Patsy is much older so the shorter run will do her good. Pull out the younger ones like Nevada, Diamond X, July, and Sundown for packhorses. You can ride Little Shot and I'll ride Jigger."

When they were about done, Deb called out, "Frying the eggs." Both stopped what they were doing and proceeded to the cookhouse. Patsy trailed along all excited, somehow knowing she was going out today.

With breakfast done and all six horses saddled and loaded, only the empty pack bags and personal gear remained. In addition to their sleeping bags, tents, small cook stove, and food in the bear-resistant container, in went the shoeing bag and the medical bag Clyde always carried with him. Clyde always told Pablo he would much rather have the medical bag and not need it than wish like heck he had brought it.

At 7:00 a.m. sharp, out the gate they went, Deb waving and shouting out, "Be careful." Dinkey was at her side, watching Patsy gloat from the back of the flatbed as they rolled by. Clyde and Pablo headed up to Courtright Lake and the Maxson trailhead, and the six hikers followed them in two cars.

At the trailhead the hikers unloaded their backpacks and Clyde delivered their wilderness permit. Then off hiking up the trail they went, waving and exchanging "See ya laters."

The pack string was on the trail an hour later. No particular hurry today, for Clyde said, "Even though this group is a good bunch of hikers, we'll still overtake them somewhere toward the top, just before the Niche. After passing them, we should arrive at their campsite about forty-five minutes before they do. Gives us enough time to unload so they will have their gear when they walk up. Patsy would prefer the slower pace too."

Partway up the trail near Chamberlain's Camp, Clyde started in again. "I remember a couple of years back, coming up the trail right here, pulling six packhorses by myself. The horses suddenly perked up their ears and all were looking forward up the trail. Thinking it might be a bear, I slowed down to keep the group tighter. Soon I heard the sound of running horses coming toward me, and I figured all heck was about to break loose. Sure enough, charging over that rise in front of us came fourteen loose horses and mules. Several had halters, and one was dragging a lead rope, but that was it. Not a single hobble or bell. The mules were the biggest problem. They blew straight for the center of my string with a challenging attitude that didn't sit well with my horses.

"I kicked my lead horse around and was able to head off the lead charging mule, going past his nose and making a tight circle with my string. I had to fight my riding horse to keep his head pointed just to the outside of the last packhorse. This was done to prevent what we call a whirlwind. To let that happen and get caught in the center could be fatal. Keeping my lead horse on the outside allows the string someplace to go but still keeps things tight and the attacking mules from getting inside the string. This gives the horses security and still allows some control of the chaos.

"Each time I made a circle and came by the lead attacking mule, he would try to bite me. He was no doubt frustrated at not being able to get into the center of the string to create havoc. As I passed, I would counter with a slap on his nose with the end of my lead rope. By the third pass, he gave up and led the loose horses and mules on down the trail toward the trailhead. I then slowed the whole show down and got 'em straight and to a stop to give them time to rest and calm down.

"Soon, all was back to normal and up the trail we went. I thought over and over where these animals would have come from but figured I would find out before the day was over. Even though none of the horses or mules had brands, I was sure I had seen most of them before. That's when I remembered a trip the prior year.

"I was overnighting at a lake called Lower Indian. It's just above the lake we're going to today. I had all my animals hobbled and belled for the night, camp was set, and I was just relaxing and enjoying the setting sun creep up the western slope of the granite of Mount Henry. You remember me telling you about Joseph Henry before. Anyway, I started hearing people talking. I walked out on a small rock outcrop and could hear them clearly then. One of 'em was commenting that there was no sign of anybody being here for at least ten years and they were way back in the boondocks. I chuckled, thinking I had just come up the same trail with seven horses less than three hours before. Don't know how they could have missed that. I kept my silence and, after finally catching their attention, simply waved.

"The parade that proceeded in front of me was like nothing I'd seen before. About half were leading one packhorse each and the other half had only their saddle horses. Hanging from all the saddles were huge rolled bundles, on each side and off the back. Two of 'em had full backpacks hanging by a hay string tied to the saddle horns. These were swinging and banging against the horses' shoulders with each step. Obviously, the rider was wearing his backpack at the start but decided to walk instead.

"The whole procession looked like a Leaning Tree cartoon. I didn't notice any marks on the animals and nothing was limping so I didn't intervene. If there was ever a sign of amateurs, this was it. Well, I just took in a deep sigh and returned to camp. The next morning I was long gone when the sun came over the mountains.

"So, remembering this, I thought they might just be the same group, since it was about the same time of the year. Just before getting to the Post Corral Creek crossing, a lone rider came up the trail toward me. By the dejected look on his face, I figured he drew the short straw to go looking for the horses. The only odd thing was he didn't have a single head rope with him. Don't know how he intended to string 'em back to camp.

"He stepped his horse off the trail, and we both stopped. I asked if he was looking for a loose herd, and he responded with only a nod. I then tore into him with how irresponsible his wilderness horse-handling skills were. Not a single one of the animals had a hobble. Allowing them to get out of his control put everyone down the trail in serious risk, and could cause resource damage due to switchback cutting by the uncontrolled loose animals. That type of behavior gives all commercial packers a bad name. Even though the animals were private stock, we are guilty by association in the eyes of the public. All those animals are no doubt at the parking lot by now and heading down the paved road. They may not even stop until the city limits of Fresno.

"I told him that I had radioed the US Forest Service Law Enforcement with a heads-up about the public safety situation. And I also told him I'd bet he was the same group camping at Lower Indian Lake that I had seen last year. With a slight nod, this guy just kept his head down and took it. I figured he had had enough and nudged my horse to get moving and off we went. I heard he finally got all of 'em gathered up and back to his camp, about four days later."

The duo crossed Post Corral Creek and headed up toward the Niche and Red Mountain Basin. "Well, the very next year, which would be last year, Deb and I were coming down this very same trail when we encountered the same group again," Clyde continued. "This time there was a big improvement in the packing gear. All brand-new and decorated with fancy silver conchos. However, all had stopped and had a forlorn look on their faces. Turns out, one of them leading a pack mule was in a hurry through a particularly rough place and the mule broke his leg. The group leader said the mule was being taken about a quarter of a mile away from the trail to be put down. About then, we heard two loud rifle shots. There was nothing left to be said. Clearly, some people refuse to learn. More interested in show than substance.

"We continued down the trail, but before passing the whole group, the last member started talking to Deb. I was right behind her and had to stop when she did. He was one of those macho, chest-pounder types with a big hat. Looking down his nose at Deb as if thinking, what's a woman doing up here in a man's world. He then glanced down at our horses' feet and said, 'Whooo does your horse shooing?' Then he spit out a stream of tobacco juice and said, 'I see only six nails per shoe. Eeeverybody knows ya need eight when doin' it proper.'

"Even though I was right behind her, I didn't feel the need to speak up. Deb, after glancing down at the rider's horse and noticing one of the shoes was missing, responded. 'Well, true cowboys know

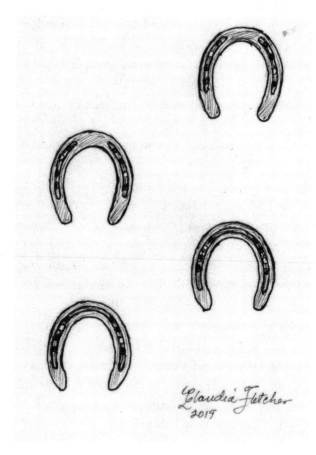

Horseshoes

80

six nails put in correctly hold just as well as eight. Also, we leave a long crimp on the nail and don't underscore the end either. This preserves full tensile strength. The nails are placed with two in the back and one on the forward nail hole on each side of each shoe. That's why these shoes stay on the horse until paper thin and never come off. It's a must riding in granite all day every day. By doing this, we've never had a sore-footed animal.' Seeing there was not going to be a response, Deb said, 'Now, I have a question for you. Whooo does your muuuule killlling?'

"I could only keep my head down to prevent the rider from seeing the grin on my face. The rider only had an open mouth with not a sound coming out. Deb then nudged her horse, and our whole string continued down the trail."

Topping out over the Niche, the group went on into Red Mountain Basin and Rae Lake. Pablo then turned in his saddle and called back to Clyde, "How often do you have to use your medical bag?"

"Well," Clyde responded, "more often than you think. It seems almost half of the injuries I see up here are foot or ankle related. Reasonable since most are walking. Often when I have come upon hikers, sitting on rocks or logs with their shoes off, I don't even have to ask what the problem is. Being up here for forty years and in a podiatric medical practice for almost forty-five years, I've about seen it, all over and over. Sometimes it's the fracture of a toe, an ingrown toenail, or blisters and such. I always stop and let them know who I am and if I can help. The look of gratitude I get is well worth any inconvenience to me. When I pull out my bag and go to work, they seem to think I was an angel from heaven. Just being practical, getting them fixed up here on the trail can literally save their trip. Otherwise, down the hill they would go and wait in a hospital ER for someone like me anyway. Might as well stop and take care of it here on the spot and save their trip.

"Every so often the issues are bigger. I remember several years ago, a call came over the radio about a young man over at Rae Lake. Right where we are headed today. I was over the hill almost to the Kings River. Seems he had a case of high-altitude pulmonary edema. HAPE for short. These are life threatening, and more than half are fatal. The leader had hiked out all night and called for help first thing in the morning. Being up at 10,000 feet and out overnight, I feared this was most likely a fatal case. I responded back to the Forest Service I was about twenty minutes from the victim and would respond back when on-site. Deb was with me. We both got on horses and double-timed it over the pass to the south and arrived at Rae Lake in about twenty-two minutes.

"Walking up to his tent, I honestly expected to find a body. Instead, he was still breathing and could respond to name and location. His lips and fingertips were purple, and he was coughing up pink pulmonary fluid, but, amazingly, he was alive and coherent. I radioed the Forest Service dispatch and got a helicopter to come in for his evacuation. The Highway Patrol helicopter arrived with EMS personnel. They had a pulse oximeter on board the helicopter. This device determines the amount of oxygen in your blood flow. Normal is 100 percent at sea level. I placed the device on my finger to get a control reading and mine was 98 percent, which is good for 10,000 feet. I suggested we place it on the pilot, but he laughingly refused, saying most likely they would ground him on the spot.

"Anyway, we then placed it on the young man and his read 58 percent. Logic says he shouldn't even be alive let alone coherent. Sometimes the young and athletic can compensate well. We then placed him on oxygen with a nasal cannula set at six. Then with assistance, we walked him to the helicopter, seated him upright, strapped him in, and off he went. Took him down to Clovis Hospital, next to Fresno, where he was admitted.

"Three days later, he walked out of the hospital fully recovered. I didn't hear from him again, until several years later when I got a phone call and it was this same young man. Said he finally found me via the internet and wanted to say hello. He explained that while waiting all night in the tent up at the lake, he felt for sure he was about to die. You are aware all the time, because with HAPE you slowly suffocate to death while your lungs fill with fluid. He was reflecting that even though he was young, he hadn't really done anything with his life. But he specifically wanted to tell me that when he saw me riding in on a horse, being a doctor and helping him out of the near-fatal situation, he realized just then what he wanted to do. This young man was proud to tell me that he was about to enter medical school at the University of Southern California and was going to specialize in emergency medicine.

"After some small talk, I just said I was glad to be of some help, wished him luck, and to keep in touch. So you see, Pablo, you never know what's around the corner going down the trail of life. The issue is not what dilemma confronts you, what matters is how you handle it. Keep your head on a swivel, ask a lot of questions, get as much education as you can from any and all sources, and be ready to act whenever adverse situations arise."

At Rae Lake the string went around to the backside and up in the trees to find the predetermined campsite. Clyde and Pablo unloaded the horses and just hung around the lake, waiting for the hikers to arrive before leaving for their own overnight campsite. Clyde chimed up again.

"Pablo, this lake was named in about 1945 after Rae Crabtree. Rae was the owner of the pack station before me. He had the station here for almost forty years. Then came a lady by the name of Bea Wright. She had it from about 1970 until I bought it from her in 1980.

"Up over there, above that granite cliff area is Dale Lake. Named after John Dale back in 1936. He was a packer out of Dinkey Creek. Up behind Dale Lake is Diamond X Lake. That was the name of the pack station John Dale owned. Over to the left and down at the bottom of that granite slide is Davis Lake. Named by John Dale after Bill Davis, who was a sheepman in this basin back then. You already know about Fleming Lake, named after another old-time sheepman here. Over there, up high, you remember Red Mountain and to the right is Hell For Sure Pass.

"As I said before, the boundary to Kings Canyon Park is there. It was named by Joseph Le Conte. He crossed it in 1904. The lake below it on this side was given the same name in 1953. Way over to the right is Devils Punchbowl Lake. Given that name by the US Geological Survey in 1907. In between Devils Punchbowl and Hell For Sure Lakes is Black Rock Lake. Heard a story back in the 1950s or '60s that a helicopter plowed to the ground right next to the lake. Crashed and burned and all four aboard died. I looked around the site and could still see the burned-out trees. Kinda looks like a regular lightning strike. Found some pieces of old foam used in the seats, but otherwise nothing. Over this hill and across from Fleming Lake, which we went by on our way here, are the slight remains of a trapper cabin. Can barely make it out, almost completely returned to nature. The trapper was named Shorty Lovelace. I'll tell you more about him later. Here come the hikers."

After they set up camp with the sound of the grazing horses' bells off in the trees, Pablo had quiet time. Sitting by Fleming Creek, drinking water he retrieved with his cup, and petting Patsy, he never felt more relaxed. He was getting into shape now, and the ride in had little to no effect on him.

The bright colors of the phlox plants along the drier rocky areas gave life to the backdrop of gray granite. At the meadow's edge he noticed the small purple tubular flowers seemly coming straight up out of the ground. The field guide that Clyde had given him told him those were most likely Sierra gentian. Looking up into the drier rocky area, he noticed some rose-colored, more-woody-type plants. He figured these to be penstemons. He glanced up near the water's edge and noticed some taller reddish flowering plants. He squatted down, and with his field guide open, he figured these might be columbine plants. He then noticed a small bunch of plants with cupped rose-pink flowers. Studying them required lying down, what Clyde called "belly botany." The field guide indicated these were pussy paws, which are found all over the high and dry areas of these Sierras. Over in another direction,

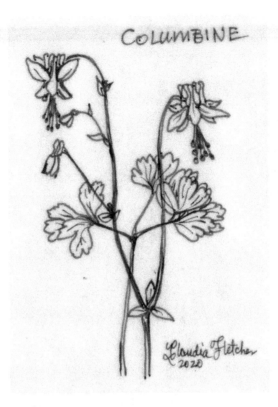

COLUMBINE

Claudia Fletcher
2020

he sighted a taller plant with six yellowish parts to the flower all in a cluster. They looked bright and cheerful to him, and he was delighted that they were probably the aptly named pretty faces in the field guide.

Starting back to camp, he stopped, for up a small draw, with good water running through it, was a group of large-leafed plants. They looked like lettuce. He reached up to take one of the flat leaves but was froze when Clyde's voice interrupted his focus.

"Don't even think about eating that plant. It's called corn lily. Looks inviting, but it's full of alkaloids and is poisonous. Indians called this high Sierra toilet paper. It's the only use worth considering. Come on, dinner is hot."

The two plus Patsy moseyed back to camp and were met with an inviting aroma as they approached. After dinner, Pablo lay in his screen-roofed tent, captivated by the stars that jumped out. He

CORN LILY

Claudia Fletcher
2020

knew a shooting-star show was coming up but not until August. He was early for that, but all the names of the stars were an overwhelming mystery to him. Pablo thought he had some idea of the layout from down in the Central Valley, but up here they came seemingly out of nowhere and totally covered the night sky. He remembered what Clyde had told him about no light pollution up in the mountains, but the sight never diminished his wonder. Soon the rhythmic breathing sounds of Patsy at the base of the lodgepole just outside his tent rocked him to sleep.

Pablo awoke with the first faint glimmer of early morning light. Hearing the distant bells on the horses comforted him.

Yep, I'm getting the hang of this, he thought. He could barely see Clyde's hands sticking out the door of his small tent about twenty feet away. Clyde was pumping up the single-burner stove to get coffee started, not even getting out of his sleeping bag. The art of making cowboy coffee was not to be hurried. The slow roll boil was the secret and forced one to take the necessary time. No rush today, since they were going out empty with no particular schedule. Even Patsy knew the schedule for today. She didn't budge. Pablo knew she was still alive since her eyes were following every move he and Clyde made.

When Clyde determined the coffee was ready, he simply gave Pablo a slight head shake, indicating time to get up. After both had crawled out of their tents and had full coffee cups in hand, Pablo figured it was time to go get the horses. Clyde stopped him and said, "Just finish a cup or two. Sit and listen to the morning wake up. The horses aren't going anywhere. Can you hear what the bells are telling you about the horses? With the slow, shallow, and intermittent clank, you are being told all is good. They're not even eating, just standing around burping and talking politics. If you hear all the bells go loud and crazy, something is spooking them and it's time to go check it out. Things were calm all night, just as they are now. The horses will be rested, full, and ready to go."

After two cups, Clyde motioned it was time to get to work. Walking out to the horses took only five minutes. Going around the backside first, putting the string together, and pulling off the hobbles went smoothly. The horses were across the creek and would have to be led back. Clyde said, "Just hop on Little Shot and ride her bareback. Ya only need the lead rope for a rein and can pull the whole string across the creek without getting your feet wet."

Back at camp, they started saddling up. Things seemed to go much faster on these last few trips and required very little instruction. Pablo felt confident he was getting the hang of the routine and wondered if Clyde would ever let him go out alone. The idea made him suddenly shudder, realizing the awesome responsibility that

Hobbled Horse with Bell

would go along with that. He knew right then that he needed more time, and he was happy he didn't ask. It took decades for Clyde and Deb to have this process down pat, and Pablo had every intention of taking his time and absorbing everything like a sponge. After the horses were checked for shoes and the saddling was finished and loaded, they were soon on their way.

Coming up to the exit stream of Fleming Lake, Clyde made a sharp left turn off the trail. He turned in the saddle and said, "Gonna show you something." Riding only a short distance they came upon a ground-level rectangle outline of rotten logs. Only one log high all the way around this tiny structure was all that remained. Even that was barely visible.

"This was once a trapper cabin. Shorty Lovelace made it. I told you I would tell you about him, and now is as good a time as any. I never met him, since he passed away quite a while ago. He started trapping over in what is now Kings Canyon National Park. When that area became a national park, he had to leave and thus came over here. He was actively trapping from about 1912 until 1961 and was the first nonnative year-round person up here. At least according to record.

"All his cabins were about this same size, roughly five feet by seven feet. They all had dirt floors. In each was a small stone fireplace with a flat metal plate on top. A round hole was cut in one end of the plate where he attached a stovepipe on up through the roof. A flat piece, usually an olive oil can, was used as the flange through the roof opening so as not to catch the roof on fire. The stovepipe was removed when not in use so it wouldn't get flattened by the winter snow.

"All of the cabins were short. The door was usually no more than three or four feet high. You or I would have to almost crawl in. Shorty would only have to duck down. I hear he was about five

SHORT'S TRAPPER CABIN

Shorty's Trapper Cabin

feet nothing on a good day. His bed was always sideways, so that's why the width was that length. Usually had two or three shelves, stocked with jars of raisins, matches, oatmeal, tea, etcetera. Always some dry wood inside too. Outside, he would have almost a cord of wood piled up and split shakes covering it.

"He had over twenty of these over in Kings Canyon, but when it became a national park, he had to move. I think he built another twenty over here. Most are like this, almost completely gone, but some are still standing. As we move around these mountains on various trips, I'll show ya. This country gets over fifteen feet of snow some winters. So, you can imagine what it would look like in the middle of winter. There would be no way you would ever find them unless you knew exactly where they were. Then when he arrived at the site, he would have to dig down until he found it. Then crawl down inside and get his stovepipe set up before he could settle in.

"Each cabin was about one day of snowshoe or ski travel apart. If the dictionary needed a picture of tough, I'm sure his would be the one they'd pick. The way he got started, I was told, was the family wanted to get him away from outside influences. Seems his brothers were well-educated engineers, responsible for many bridge projects in the area, and Shorty was an embarrassment. Apparently, Shorty had a drinking problem. Deb's father had met him several times over in Visalia. None of those times was Shorty sober.

"The family would bankroll him in the fall to get stocked up with provisions in all these cabins. An old cowboy I mentioned earlier, Bob Simmons, used to pack in his provisions during the fall. Frequently, after the provisions were placed in the cabin, there was only enough room for Shorty to squeeze in and that was it. Apparently, he did quite well as a trapper. At the time, when the average intake was less than $500 for the season, Shorty would average about $2,000. It's strange, after all the fuss the family went through to get rid of him so as not to diminish the family name, Shorty is the only one in the family that everyone remembers and writes about. Most of the writing was done about his time in the

Kings Canyon National Park. Namely by a park historian, William Tweed. Nothing I know of has been written about his time here. Maybe someday I'll tackle that project."

Heading back down and passing the Niche, Clyde started in again. "Pablo, I remember a time Deb and I dropped off a group at this place. It was during an approaching thunderstorm. See those old trees over there, all twisted and the tops gone? Lightning has just been beating the crap out of them. This ridge is high and exposed, a perfect setup for frequent strikes.

"After the group was off the horses, gear unloaded, horses restrung together and ready to head home, the leader wanted all to stand still so he could get a picture. I advised that's not a good idea, as we'd better get going fast. He replied with don't worry, it will be OK. He didn't get the last word out when we got hit no more than fifty feet away. It is so fast, like flash-boom, as if one word. Sounds like somebody shooting a .30-06 off in your ear. That made believers out of all of 'em. We scattered like quail. They flew up the trail to Red Mountain, Deb and I went down as fast as we could. See that burn hole in the tree up there on the left. That's where it hit. Didn't kill the tree but blew bark and dust all over. The air smelled like burnt ozone."

After crossing Post Corral Creek and getting on the final leg back to the trailhead, Clyde pointed off to the right. "Across the creek and up the hill a ways is another of Shorty's cabins. I'll take you there on another trip. As you can see, it's about the maximum for one-day travel during winter, especially if you had to go uphill. Like I said, he left here in 1961 and two years later he died. Maybe he should never have left."

The whole remaining ride out, all Pablo could think of was Shorty's picture in the dictionary next to the word *tough*.

CHAPTER 6

Trail Trip

"Wake up, Pablo. Time's a wastin'. Got a big trip ahead and a lot of work to get started," Clyde hollered from out on the loading dock.

Pablo was soon arriving, coffee cup in hand and with a big yawn. "We got all this equipment to get loaded, about eight packhorses' worth. Going out for eight days on a trail-clearing trip," Clyde continued. "The US Forest Service has provided four seasonal employees for this venture. I provided a cook. He's right over there; name's Robert Golden. Robert came in late last night with a truck full of food and kitchen equipment. The Forest Service personnel will be here shortly.

"This whole trip has taken years to formulate. For years, the Forest Service has been hauling in the trail crew, simply dropping them off and leaving. They then had to walk out each day and with handsaws commence clearing logs from the trail, then hike back to camp. Each day the walk got farther and farther to the worksite, all on the clock. I've always felt this inefficiency was incredibly wasteful.

"As you can imagine the work production got steadily less as each day went on during the tour due to the backtrack hiking required. Was always told by Forest Service managers, they didn't think the crew would want to move camp all the time. I repeatedly told them to just directly ask the crew and you would find out different. That seemed to be too much trouble for the managers. This coming from top-level people, who virtually never come out into the wilderness themselves but think they know best. The ground troops could only shrug their shoulders and continue to say what can they do. Most of these trail crew members have college degrees of their own but are at the bottom of the totem pole and were only being ignored.

"Seeing the reroute damage the public did by having to go around these obstacles for no sound reason, only ego, just infuriated me. I finally had to volunteer with all the packing, livestock, food, and cook to get this approved. All the Forest Service had to do was provide the four trail personnel, who are already on the clock anyway. Almost took an act of Congress to get the thumbs-up.

"It's been one heck of a winter and trees are down like matchsticks all over the wilderness trail system. Would take 'em five years at the old rate to maybe get caught up. Also, the Wilderness Act has a provision that allows the Forest Service personnel to use chainsaws, but prior approval is required. You rarely see this because it's amazing how mid- to upper-level managers can inject their personal agendas and subject all the workers and public to submit to their interpretation. Over time, the public and the wilderness itself suffer. This lack of efficiency is costly. Their only answer was just 'Give us more money and we've always done it this way.' Well, that doesn't sit well with me, especially in today's world.

"Anyway, two weeks ago, we finally got written approval for the chainsaws for Forest Service use in the wilderness for this trip, on any tree where safety was a concern. That is monumental in itself. If we can pull this off like I think we can, history will be made, and hopefully we'll get the top-level supervisors to change their way of thinking.

"All four of the trail crew are walking, so all we need are the eight packhorses and saddle horses for the three of us. Go pull out Poco, Diamond X, Nosebag, Valor, Loper, Pearl, July, and Sundown. When you get them up to the hitching rail, go get Camp for Robert and Jay for yourself, and I'll take Chowchilla. Meanwhile, Robert and I will be packing the pannier loads. We have sixteen of 'em, so we are gonna be busy for awhile."

After about an hour, the pack loads were about done, and all eleven horses were saddled. Deb called out, "Frying the eggs," and the three stopped work and went into the cookhouse. About twenty minutes later, they emerged to resume the work when the trail crew showed up. Their names were Josh Smith, Scott Eichorn, Anthony LeLuca, and Pierre Perrilion. Pierre was from France, finishing the last of his university degree and here as a summer employee. The other three were regular seasonal employees with many years' experience. Josh, the leader, explained to Clyde that his boss had directed him to finish on time as there was no budget for even a minute of overtime. Clyde nodded, then looked over their personal gear and trail tools and confidently declared we're good with the eight packhorses. "Let's finish loading up, head out, and go make history." Dinkey jumped in Clyde's flatbed at the last minute.

The haul took both trucks with trailers, since both flatbeds were needed to transport the gear to the trailhead. After the fifteen-minute drive to Woodchuck trailhead, the horses were unloaded and packed up. The four trail crew members started out up the trail, carrying a chainsaw and a six-foot two-person handsaw called a misery whip, plus an ax, water, and lunch. This was early in the summer, and few people would be in the backcountry. The time of year was chosen to minimize the impact of the chainsaw noise on wilderness travelers. The pack string was to follow, overtake, and pass the trail crew and proceed on to the first preselected camp spot for the evening, Moore Boys Meadow. This location had good feed and water, and, most important, was a convenient stopping point for the trail crew workday.

It didn't take long before Clyde, Pablo, and Robert encountered two of the trail crew. Only about a half mile up the trail was the first tree. The trail crew determined the misery whip could handle it, so the other two went on up the trail to the next worksite. Having two groups of two was working out well, since they could

String of Eight

simply leapfrog each other. Getting the pack string around the tree wasn't much trouble and onward they went. Shortly, the three could hear the whine of a chainsaw up ahead. Sure enough, two huge red fir trees were crisscrossed in the middle of the trail. One was suspended in the air. This was an extremely dangerous situation, so everyone was glad to have the chainsaw. Negotiating around these downfalls was more difficult but was accomplished. Clyde always told Pablo, "Just pause a moment to pick your route and take it easy. Once you are committed with a long pack string, generally turning around is not an option."

After crossing Woodchuck Creek—quite high owing to early-season runoff—they proceeded up the trail paralleling the creek. They encountered numerous switchbacks, but Clyde said they were not a big deal and kept the string connected. Topping over a rise, the three could see Moore Boys Meadow, and Clyde proceeded to the west side where they found good tree cover. Also, this location was on the opposite side of the meadow from the trail.

Unloading the eight packhorses went much faster than the earlier load-up. Robert went to work setting up the kitchen and starting dinner. Pablo and Clyde unsaddled the packhorses and two of the saddle horses. Clyde kept his saddled. He told Pablo to help Robert and then went up trail to scout the tree damage and estimate the workload for the next day. Both groups of the trail crew had radios that Clyde owned. They were instructed to use Clyde's channel so as to not interfere with any Forest Service radio traffic. This was most useful for safety and practicality, because Robert would know when to expect everyone in for dinner. As it worked out, both trail groups and Clyde arrived back at camp right at 5:00 p.m.

Pablo remembered this location from a prior ride through. Clyde had told him about the Moore brothers using this as a summer cow camp. He finally got to see the remains of both the log cabins. At this time, they were barely visible as a line of wood chips and one decomposing log forming the outline of each cabin. The rock pile at their ends indicated where the stone fireplaces had been. He remembered Clyde showing him a picture a patient had brought to him. It depicted a whole herd of cattle stuffed in this meadow and smoke coming out of one of the chimneys. Clyde had said this meadow was used as a gathering location before the long drive down the mountain, which usually took about one week. The picture was dated about 1920.

The woodchucks chirping across the meadow in the rocky talus hillside let Pablo know he was invading their 'hood. Clyde had told him that these were most likely not true woodchucks but more of a rock chuck or yellow-bellied marmot. It was still fascinating to Pablo, observing the whole town come alive after only ten minutes of being still and watching.

After they had finished dinner, washed the dishes, set up the tents, and rolled out the beds, Pablo soon found himself crawling into bed, listening to the sounds of the creek and the slow ringing of the horses' bells, and dozing off to sleep. All was good.

Marmot

"Bang that coffee pot again, Robert. Pablo might hear it the third time," Clyde commanded loudly. Pablo jumped up, realizing he hadn't moved a muscle since laying his head down the evening before. It was going to take a couple of cups of cowboy coffee to get him back into this world.

Pablo crawled out of his tent after dressing, and Clyde handed him a cup that Robert then filled. Clyde started up with, "Pablo, do ya hear that sound? It's the perfect start to any wilderness packer's day. The sound of the horses' bells off in the trees. The horses didn't go far, so gulp down another cup and let's get to work. The sun is almost up."

Retrieving the eleven horses didn't take much effort, and Pablo was wide awake upon the return to camp. After all were tied up,

Clyde declared, "Robert says breakfast is ready. When he says it's time, we jump. Pablo, go tell the four that the grub is ready. Time to get them moving."

After breakfast, the trail crew headed off to work, saws in hand, lunches in pockets, and bellies full. Two of them took the north route to Woodchuck Lake and the other took the south route. Both teams would meet at the top of Crown Pass, then proceed down the other side to the North Fork of the Kings River. At that location they would camp—at Maxson Meadow. Pablo remembered going by it on a previous trip to Blackcap Basin. It was a long way for the day's trip, but Clyde said the trees were few and far between so they should make good time. The whole top part of the route was around 10,000 feet as they were getting close to timberline.

The second morning went a little faster. Robert started pairing up the pack loads as they were on the first day. Some of the loads never were opened since they contained food for the back end of the trip. After all eleven horses were saddled, Clyde and Pablo helped Robert finish setting out the pack panniers. They created two rows with each matched-up pack bag opposite the other, about six feet apart. The first packhorse, Pearl, was brought up, and while Robert held her, Pablo lifted the bag load on the right side and Clyde did the same on the left. Then Pablo picked up the folded top tarp on his side, unrolled it, and placed it over the whole top load. Clyde then tossed the lash rope cinch over the top, and Pablo then tossed it back under the animal. Clyde grabbed hold of it, ran the rope around the hook, then pulled tight, and, after placing a half-hitch knot, tossed the remaining coiled rope back over to Pablo. He then did the forward and back loops around the loads and tossed the remaining rope back to Clyde. He then did the same and secured the loose end of the rope with two half-hitches at the top and Pearl was done. This whole process took no more than eight minutes. Clyde then led Pearl over to a tie-up tree while Pablo retrieved Nosebag. After handing Nosebag to Robert, the process was repeated. The eight horses were done in about an hour and fifteen minutes. Then, after putting lunches in saddlebags and filling water bottles, they were on the trail fifteen minutes later.

"Today's ride is about five hours," Clyde explained. "Going by the overlook to Indian Spring Meadow and then over Crown Pass. Most of that is close to 10,000 feet. Looking to the west ya can see forever. Right up here we're going to stop for a few minutes, but I won't tell you why. You'll have to wait and see."

After riding about three hours, Pablo turned in the saddle and noticed a lone hiker approaching. It was obvious he was experienced since was traveling fast and light and had a determined look on his face. Clyde pulled the string over and let him pass. The hiker stopped and declared how impressed he was with the trail-clearing effort.

"Wanted you to know I shook hands and thanked each guy in that trail crew I passed a little ways back. Told 'em I know this is tough work and appreciate every bit of it."

Clyde tipped his hat and said thank you for thinking of the crew and let the hiker be on his way. He was soon around the turn in the trail, out of sight, and they never saw him again the whole trip.

After coming up to a flat granite slab, Clyde, Pablo, and Robert stopped, tied up, and walked over to the edge. Pablo couldn't believe what came into view. Down below him was the most beautiful lake surrounded by meadow he had ever seen.

"That's Crown Lake," Clyde said. "It's about ten acres but looks bigger with all that green meadow that surrounds it. This trail hugs the cliff to our left and continues over the top and down the other side to the North Fork of the Kings River. All the water from here goes toward the Middle Fork of the Kings River.

"I remember, I think it was back in 1984, a private contracted trail crew redid all this trail we've been on and up to the end just over there about a quarter mile. Cost the US Forest Service $4 per foot. Totaled about $340,000. We did all the packing for them. Took them in and out every ten days. A nice group of true

gentlemen from Oregon. Think their name was Sprague or something like that. They worked hard but ate good. We hauled in cases
of prefrozen steaks. One of 'em would dig a hole, drop the case in,
place empty burlap sacks over them, and then finish filling with
dirt. Each morning they would take out that night's steaks to thaw.
The remaining stayed frozen the whole ten days. During lunchtime
or after dinner, all they would talk about was the stock market or
golf scores. Was an extended family with grandpa, dad, and sons.
About eight in total.

"All this granite along the cliff route had to be blasted. No power
rock drill was allowed in the contract. The old grandpa was assigned
the task of hand-drilling each dynamite hole. Took two thousand
hits with a sledgehammer on a star drill for each hole. He kept at it
all day, every day, and always had a smile on his face. I wondered if
it was just a way of letting out frustration. They also did all this fill
on the downside of the trail. Placed each rock in exactly the right
position according to its natural shape. After all these years, many
with deep snow, not a single one of these rocks has moved. Looks
like it was built by the Romans. Pablo, as we ride by, take a good
look, 'cause that's quality work."

Topping out over Crown Pass, Pablo looked behind him and
could see Finger Rock and Crown Rock and, looking forward,
Blackcap Peak. Way in the background was Mount Goddard. "Las
montañas son increíble, y la vista es grandioso," Pablo declared
somewhat louder than he intended. Clyde only smiled; no translation was needed for Robert.

They continued down the switchbacks on the backside toward
the upcoming view overlooking Half Moon Lake. Clyde called out,
"That lake is larger than you think. Covers over fifty acres and is one
of the biggest up here. Loaded with brook trout, but most are small.
Can catch all you want but nothing big." After they passed the
lake, the trail turned and headed down the exit stream. Then they
passed the Scepter Trail turnoff toward Blackcap, and the farther
they rode the steeper it got. After making numerous hard-left, then

hard-right turns, they finally bottomed out at Maxson Meadow, named after an early stockman. Crossing the North Fork of the Kings River was no problem since Clyde knew where the sandbars were.

After the animals were unloaded, hobbled, and turned out, Clyde took off riding up the trail to scout out the next day's work. The trail crew and Clyde kept in touch by radio. Knowing how the crew was doing and when to expect them in was always a great help and made things go much smoother.

During dinner, everyone was happy to hear Clyde's report that it would be best to spend two nights at this camp. In the morning, Clyde would ferry up the gear for two of the trail crew back toward Half Moon Lake so they could work the Scepter Trail up canyon toward Blackcap. The other two would go up this main river trail and meet up with the Scepter Trail pair at the junction. The four would stash the tools there and walk the short distance empty back to camp. Clyde said a big mess was just up the main trail and would keep 'em busy all day. The next morning the trail crew cleared the mess and got back by 5:00 p.m., the normal dinner hour. This was important since the outfit had only so much daylight to wash all the dishes and get to bed early. Everything worked out perfectly.

The following morning, the four trail crew members headed out together. One pair was to continue up to the end of the Black-cap Trail, and the other was to turn left and head up to Bench Valley. Camp was to be moved up to Bench Valley for the night. By this time Clyde, Robert, and Pablo had a routine down pat. All eight packhorses were loaded, tarps placed, and ropes lashed on and strung up, ready to go in forty-five minutes. Up the trail they went, arriving at the junction, turning left, and heading up toward Bench Valley. Both groups always maintained radio contact, so the trail crew knew the pack string was on its way to set up camp and make dinner. That was always comforting to the four.

This continued day after day like a well-oiled machine. Each day's ride had been shortened due to the volume of trees and time required to clear. Everything had to be done within a standard workday, so pacing the progress and campsite locations was extremely important.

Both Scott and Anthony were about Pablo's size. Josh, the most experienced, was an absolute string-bean type. Even though his height was about the same as Pablo's, he had to be twenty-five pounds lighter.

Pablo thought Josh's body fat was, at most, 1 percent. The cigarette that continually hung from his mouth equaled the width of his side profile. He nicknamed him Cig. Pierre was an absolute flagpole. To Pablo, Pierre was at least seven feet tall, even though he knew this was an exaggeration. Pablo thought it was OK to call him Frenchy. Pierre didn't seem to mind. All four had the stamina of Olympic athletes. Day in and day out, they carried the saws, fuel, axes, lunches, and water up and down these 9,000- and 10,000-foot trails. Pablo finally asked Clyde, "How can Josh do all that work, in this altitude, never tire, and still have a cigarette constantly hanging from his mouth?"

"That's a testimony to the human spirit," Clyde answered. "I know another gentleman who can do the same thing. His name is Jim Wagner, an attorney in town. Comes up here about twice a year. A few years ago, he pushed his autistic son in a wheelchair the entire length of the Boston Marathon. Even though I don't agree with that health habit, you have to admire the grit it takes to override and accomplish any amazing feat that extreme. In life, you will always be impressed with the inner human drive, in spite of medical obstacles, whether self-imposed or not.

"I remember another guy; I think his last name was Perko. He was a chief financial officer with San Diego schools. After an auto accident, he was paralyzed from the waist down, but the disability didn't seem to put him down, just slowed him down. He would come up here several times. After Deb and I would help him into the saddle, he would lock his leg braces and strap his crutches on the side of the saddle, much as you would a rifle. Up the trail we would go, all the way to Horsehead Lake in Bench Valley, or on a different trip we went to Pearl Lake over in Blackcap Basin. Those are each eight-hour rides, one way. I would then drop all of them off and head out the next day. I have to add that his daughter-in-law, who was a family practice doctor, always came along.

"Anyway, when I would return to pick them up, he was always excited to go over in detail all the surrounding lakes he day-tripped to during his weeklong stay. I'm still amazed at the tenacity it took to climb over all this granite, at this altitude, with crutches and leg braces, visiting all those higher lakes, and still be able to get back to camp each afternoon, unaided. Ya never know the inner strength some people have until they're tested. When you see it in pure form, no human can help but be humbled by the experience."

From camp, mid-trail along an area called Meadow Brook, two of the trail crew went north up and into an area called Red Mountain Basin. They then were to descend west down to the main trail at Post Corral Meadow. This section Pablo remembered seeing from the Niche trip. The other two went south, down to the Kings River near the Pot Holes, then west and north to meet up with their crewmates at Post Corral. Clyde had determined the workload would be about right for all to end a normal workday at this location.

Pulling in to Post Corral Meadow but before crossing the creek, they set up camp on the north side, to be as far from the trail and creek as possible. This area had been hammered by the previous winter storms. Trees were crisscrossed over the trail some five high. Pablo was amazed about how much the landscape can be modified with just one heavy winter. It was going to take almost half a day to clear this mess. Since tomorrow was the last day, everyone would have to hustle.

The sound of Robert gently banging the coffee pot came while all was still in darkness. Pablo could see Clyde and Robert around the small campfire, pouring their first cups of coffee. Dinkey was sitting at Clyde's feet, wagging her tail in anticipation of a new day.

The trail crew members were starting to stir. This was the last day of the tour, and they were eager to get at it, knowing today wasn't going to be easy.

The four trail crew members came into camp and, after piling up their sleeping bags, tents, and clothes bags, sat down for coffee and breakfast. Excitement was in the air, and even Dinkey felt it, having a higher energy level than normal. Soon, all were working and only the sounds of crosscut and chain saws could be heard. Since this was a convergence point for three trails and a first-day destination objective for overnight hikers, it was imperative to clean up the area. Not doing so would result in extreme resource damage caused by wilderness travelers.

By noon the area had been cleared. After lunch the trail crew set out toward the trailhead, working along the way. Soon the sound of the saws could be heard. Clyde said, "That didn't take long. Let's load up."

COFFEE POT

The kitchen and camping equipment always weighed the same, but the food containers were noticeably lighter. Some of the heavier items were redistributed to make all eight packhorse loads even. With the string put together and the three mounted up, the out-fit started down the last leg of the trip, Dinkey happily following. After only two hours on the trail, the trio ran into the crew working on a log nobody enjoys—a tree that falls right down the length of the trail and has to be removed. This requires multiple cuts and sectioning of the tree. Then you lever-bar each segment out and off the trail.

All four crew members were needed for this effort. Two started at each end of this four-foot-diameter proud gift of nature. About half-way through, a group of seven hikers came up the trail and stopped. Clyde motioned for all work to stop to allow the hikers to pass, but passing by was not their only intention. They had stopped to thank everyone for the herculean effort. Clyde said, "Don't thank me. They are the ones who deserve the credit," pointing to the four crew members. Pablo was impressed to see all seven hikers line up and person-ally shake hands and thank each crew member. Since the lone hiker on the first day, this was the only group of public hikers they had seen on the entire trip. Perfect way for the crew to end their tour.

The trio continued down the trail with the horse string. Com-ing upon another portion of the trail, Clyde stopped and pointed out to Pablo, "See these cut sections of a tree rolled out off the trail? Well, I remember when this tree was still standing. I was coming up with a load of gear for another group and ran into a Boy Scout troop stopped here for a rest. All seemed to be crowded under the downhill side of this one large, dry, and leaning tree, since it was the closest shade. I stopped and said my usual howdy-do's. Then I asked all twelve of those youngsters to look up and tell me what they observed. I said to 'em, can anybody give me two reasons why it is not a good idea to sit here. The two adult leaders just took off their hats and scratched their heads with a perplexed expression. With nothing but silence, I had to continue.

"Well, ya see those dry branches sticking out all up that trunk. Those are called widow makers. They have killed many unsuspecting folks when they snap off. Second, notice that spiral crack in the tree starting from the base and traveling all the way to the top. With the downhill lean, that tree is almost ready to go over. Wouldn't want to be under it when it does.

"You should have seen them jump and scatter like quail. I continued on after tipping my hat, wishing all a good day. That afternoon, upon my return down the mountain, I came around that turn behind us and slammed on the brakes. Right here in the trail was that massive tree. I got around it and continued. I'm sure the scout troop had to come out this way. Hope they noticed the near miss and learned from it."

The trio could hear the trail crew coming up behind them, so Clyde nudged his horse and the pack string continued. But soon the sound of the saws signaled no urgent need to move, so the group slowed down again.

At the bottom of the switchbacks where they exited the wilderness, Clyde pointed off to the right and said, "Over there is an old log cabin. It's what was left from the Chamberlain cow camp. When I first started practice, an elderly lady named Beth Chamberlain came in. She got to talking about her childhood up here during the summers. Her family built the cabin and had corrals out in front. As you can see, there's a real nice meadow the whole place overlooks. This was their gather point to get the total count before heading down the mountain in the fall.

"Told me about a time, while building the cabin, they used coiled ropes around the roof rafter logs. After many wraps of the rope, the end was thrown over the top of the cabin frame and tied off to the saddle horn on a horse on the other side. This was done on each side of the log; thus two horses were needed to pull in tandem. The idea was to pull and thus roll the log up on runners to the desired location of the roof and stop, starting with the top stringer first and working their way back down. All started out good until one of the horses spooked, making the other horse think the devil was after it. Both took off, taking the log airborne. Everyone scattered, knowing for certain that disaster was coming. Well, when the log hit the ground on the other side it became a brake. Both horses stopped and started eating the grass in front of 'em, repeatedly lifting their heads and wondering what all the human fuss was about. Beth's father just said, 'Let's just put the horses on the other side of the cabin and go in the opposite direction, since the log is already over here.' That seemed to work, and all went well thereafter. The cabin still stands as you see it today."

Finally arriving at the Courtright trailhead, Pablo noticed the Forest Service truck and one of Clyde's rigs, which had already been shuffled to this spike station. Deb was waiting with the second rig and wearing a smile. The eight horses were unloaded onto the loading dock and divided into the two trailers. About then the trail crew came into view. Clyde looked down at Deb's watch and noticed he had two minutes to spare.

Gathering the whole group, Clyde said, "Gentlemen, you've just completed clearing one hundred miles of trail and cut over two hundred trees. With the old method, this would have taken four or five years at best. You all did it in eight days. Congratulations, ya just made history."

CHAPTER 7

Bench Valley

Pablo had been waking up a little earlier each day lately, and this day was no exception. He was delighted when he glanced out the window while opening the bunkhouse door and saw Clyde walking past with his coffee cup in hand. There was no need for Clyde to holler for him to wake up, since he was dressed and on his way before the sun was up. Clyde raised his cup with a slight gesture and head nod for Pablo to get his filled as well as to get to work. Not a word was spoken. Clyde continued on to the corral, with a slight smile, thinking this kid is catching on.

"Where to today?" Pablo asked after returning from the cookhouse.

"Heading up to Bench Valley today. Got a group of nine people. Three riders and the others are walkers. It's an eight-hour ride in, one way, and the leader wanted everyone to get there in one day. The walkers are lean and fit, but no way would the older three make it in one day. They range in age from eighty-one to eighty-four years old. It would take them probably three days for the trip in alone.

"The three of us will spend the night in the area and come out tomorrow. We'll do the same for their return trip, going in one day early so they can be loaded up early and on the trail before 9:00 a.m. It's the only way to get 'em out in a working day and back before dark.

"The leader is a recently retired ranger from the US Forest Service over in the Inyo National Forest. All the others are members of his family. The riders are a grandpa and two great-uncles of his. Looks like we will need five packhorses for their gear and one for ours. For their three riding horses, pull out Howdy, Spice, and Cowgirl. Then get the six packhorses. Take Diamond X, Nosebag, Valor, Poco, Loper, and July. I'll ride Jigger, Deb will take Little Shot, and you can grab Jay. When all twelve are at the hitching rail, we can start saddling."

After going through the corral gate and wading into the horse herd, Pablo asked, "Why are we taking Valor as a packhorse? You usually ride her."

"Yeah, that's true. But when you have a large group, it's best to have at least one animal in the packhorse string that can go either way, saddle or pack. That way, if there's any problem with a saddle horse, we have a backup with us and can change out and nobody has to walk. Better to have that option and not need it than to wish like heck we had thought of it earlier."

That all made sense to Pablo as he was putting on halters and snapping lead ropes. Clyde had always said to focus on what you're doing at the moment but think about the future. Anticipating problems around the next turn in the trail of life means you have plan B and plan C at the ready and can instantly adjust. Being prepared costs virtually nothing, but it can pay off big time by avoiding lost time and hassle and, once in a while, save a life.

About halfway through the saddling process, Deb called out, "Frying the eggs." The two stopped and proceeded to the cookhouse with Dinkey and Patsy following along, all excited with anticipation.

As Clyde and Pablo were coming back from breakfast, they saw the group was just starting to put their gear on the loading dock. Clyde motioned to Pablo to finish saddling and he would start packing the loads. Deb soon arrived after washing dishes, making lunches, and cleaning up the kitchen. Soon the twelve animals were loaded into the two gooseneck trailers and the twelve individual full pack bags were divided up between the two flatbeds and loaded. The vehicles started a slow roll out of the compound, and Dinkey and Patsy each picked a flatbed and hopped in. The clients followed in their cars, and the whole procession left headquarters, caravan style.

"Out the gate," Clyde called to Pablo. Looking at his watch, Pablo noted, yet again, it was 7:00 a.m. sharp. He then asked Clyde why he always said the same phrase as they leave headquarters.

"Don't know. Ever since I heard it at a horse racetrack, I always felt it had a nice ring to it. Even though we are at a turtle's pace, the general idea is the same."

Loading up at the Maxson trailhead by Courtright Lake went routinely. The walking portion of the group waved good-bye and headed up the trail. Soon, Deb had fitted the riders to their saddles, packed lunches in saddlebags, and tied jackets to the backs of the saddles. She completed the basic riding instructions and the bee drill. The two-way radios were turned on and checked. Clyde and Deb exchanged a kiss. Then she, with the riders and Patsy following, started up the trail.

Pablo was again reminded of the serious responsibility Deb had, taking care of other humans riding on live animals in a wilderness filled with surprises, both wanted and unwanted. He knew it would be a long time before he felt comfortable undertaking that assignment.

After the hour it took to load the six packhorses, Clyde and Pablo mounted their horses and followed up the trail with Dinkey in the lead. Clyde did the usual radio call to Deb, just to check in and let her know they were on our way. Deb called back saying all was good on the switchbacks before the Hobler Lake turnoff and she had not yet passed the hikers. Knowing where each other was at all times was a great comfort to all and everyone could then settle in for the day's ride. Pablo knew frequent radio check-ins between Clyde and Deb would take place throughout the day until they caught up with each other.

Not far after leaving the trailhead, Clyde called to Pablo, "I remember a few years ago an extended family of about twelve wanted to go down to a favorite secret camping place down on the Kings River. It's not too far down off to our right. All cross country and takes about two hours to get there. About half is nice and gentle, but the other half is almost at a 45-degree pitch down to the river and again back up on the return. The family always walked, but that year they decided old granddad was too old to walk the whole way and wanted him taken in on horseback. He was about eighty-eight years old, an attorney who had taught many decades at Boalt Hall law school in Berkeley. I explained when they booked that I could only get them to within three hundred yards of their camp, for after that the granite was too steep for the horses and he would have to walk. The granddad said that was OK, since he had walked it many times and the last part would be a piece of cake. He had arranged for the grandkids to be available to transport his gear from the drop-off point down to camp, and I could just turn around.

"The family carried their own backpacks but did give me some extra food to take in along with granddad's gear. To be extra cautious, Deb went with me on the trip. We put him on an older horse named Cherokee, who was a narrow Arab, and that made it easier on an old person's hips. We also put him in an old packer saddle. It, too, was narrow and had a high front fork and rear cantle. These features helped to keep him in the saddle over steep terrain. I led with the packhorse and kept a slow pace so Cherokee would have no trouble staying right behind me.

"Deb was right behind the granddad and able to keep a sharp eye on him. Down and down we went. Even though I hadn't been down there in about ten years, finding the best route wasn't all that difficult. Popping out at the granite area we stopped and unloaded granddad. There were no grandkids at the site, and I didn't feel good about just turning around so I decided to keep his gear on the pack-horse and proceed down the remaining portion, get the grandkids to head back up, and help granddad down. Deb stayed with the client and I headed down, first side-hilling, then picking a safe route before starting the last part down. Looking back, I saw granddad following me. He said he didn't want to be a bother since he had been this way many times.

"Coming to a flat place, we both stopped and could see camp through the trees. We also could hear the chatter from the remaining part of the group. Granddad said he could handle it from here since this was the easy part and for me to go on and connect with the group to unload the packhorse. He then thanked me for going the extra effort to get his gear all the way to camp and to thank Deb for all her effort.

"After completing the remaining ride down to camp, unloading, and getting ready to start back, I noticed no granddad. Instead of just leaving, something told me to go and check it out and make sure he joined his group. One of the grandsons was standing with me. I directed him to come with me so when we found granddad, he could walk him back the remaining short distance to camp.

"Off we went. We found granddad less than a hundred yards from camp. He had stepped over a log and fallen. Looking at his left ankle, I could see it was obviously broken. Well, we are two hours, cross country, from any trail and down in a steep canyon. I was able to call out to the US Forest Service dispatcher to get a helicopter evacuation started. Within fifteen minutes the evacuation helicopter was overhead and lowering the line with the equipment bag attached. This was necessary since there was no place for the airship to land. The EMS person on board knew I was a doctor, and that eliminated the need for her to be lowered down to get granddad ready to hoist. The vacuum splints provided were for a forearm, so I had to improvise with a double-up to get from his toes to as high up his leg as I could. Also, since the splints were narrow, I had to secure them in place with tape, at the forefoot, mid-foot, lower leg, and upper leg. Again, you have to work with what you have and make it happen.

"There was an overhanging dead tree directly above us, so after his ankle was secure, we had to move him about thirty feet over. Would have been ugly for him to get hung up fifty feet in the air.

Next came the harness. I had to fit it around both legs and arms and across his chest. Then came the last step of attaching a carabiner clip to the keeper-hook at the end of the lift line. With this done, I was able to give the all-good-to-go over the radio directly to the pilot and up he went. I'm not going to lie and say I wasn't nervous about that carabiner holding. If that failed and he dropped from a hundred feet, it would not have been a pretty sight. Having that happen to this high-profile attorney definitely wouldn't have made my day, let alone his.

"Anyway, all went well and off he went to Community Regional Medical Center Trauma Unit in Fresno. I found out later, his ankle was put back together, and he was picked up by his wife and on the way home in two days. I was able to report this back to the group when I went back in, five days later, to bring out some gear. They were glad they had listened to granddad's wish and stayed to enjoy the entire trip.

"Deb and I originally thought we would be out by early afternoon that day. It was way after dark before we even got back to the trailhead. I'm just glad I followed a hunch and stuck around. If I had left after the drop-off, they would have been in a much more serious fix. So, Pablo, in the wilderness, always err on the side of caution. More often than not, you'll be darn glad you did."

Onward Pablo and Clyde marched, keeping up a good pace to catch up to Deb as soon as possible. After the turnoff to Hobler Lake, Clyde talked to Deb via the radio. They were able to determine the pack string was gaining fairly fast. The going is always much slower with clients riding, and Pablo realized how much faster everything went by having Deb leave early with the riders. If they had waited at the trailhead until everything was loaded and left together, the whole procession would have been an hour later getting started. With eight hours of riding, any time saved by using a different system means not having to set up camp in the dark.

Crossing Post Corral Creek, the string paused to let the horses drink. Clyde spoke up. "Pablo, I remember a time when old man

Bob Chasing Bear

Bob Simmons ran cattle around here. A group of campers was sitting around their tents right over there across the meadow. I was here with a pack string, doing just what we're doing now, letting 'em drink. I think I was on my way through to Blackcap, but anyway, I heard a faint holler way off upstream in the trees. The campers didn't notice at first. This hollering kept getting louder and louder. Finally, those campers noticed and were all looking in the same direction off to the tree line. Then bam, out of the trees came a black bear running at full speed across the meadow and toward the campers at the other side. Right behind him was Ol' Bob Simmons on his horse and hollering at the top of his voice. Nothing in particular, just "Hee-haw!" Over his head he was swinging his rope. He was trying to lasso the bear. I guess the bear was heading for the campers for protection from this wild man.

"You should have seen those campers scatter like a covey of quail. Screaming and just running for their lives, totally convinced they were about to be future bear crap. Halfway across the meadow, Bob suddenly saw me and pulled up. The bear continued on to the other side of the meadow and disappeared into the trees. Bob just waved to me with a grin on his face, turned his horse, and slowly trotted on back the way he came in. For some reason, my horses didn't get excited, and I guess Bob, seeing me there, didn't want to push the prank. I continued to let the horses finish drinking and then proceeded on across and toward Blackcap. I didn't see Bob or any of the campers again, and they were long gone when I came back through the next day. Never found out what Bob intended to do with the bear if he actually caught it. He has long since passed away so I guess I'll never find out."

After about an hour, the packhorse string caught up with Deb and the client riders. They had stopped at the Pot Holes on the Kings River to take a short lunch break. They still had not passed any of the hikers in the group. Clyde noticed one of the client riding horses needed a left front shoe, so he took this break to do some replacement shoeing. Dinkey and Patsy were enjoying the rest, sound asleep under fir trees after dipping in the river pools.

Thirty minutes later everyone was ready to get the second half of the ride under way. After getting the three elderly clients on the riding horses, Clyde led the way pulling the pack string, followed by Pablo with the one packhorse. Then came the clients, and Deb was at the end. Deb was grateful for the change in position. She could now keep a good eye on the clients without having to constantly turn around in the saddle. For the clients, Clyde's pace was faster than it was during the first half, and they soon noticed the increased pace of their riding horses without having to nudge them at all.

They soon turned left, away from the river, and started uphill. This was a much faster and safer route. "Deb and a prior employee named Stephanie Wright scouted out this new route up to Bench Valley," Clyde said. "It was necessary so I could get the paraplegic named Perko, who I told you about before, up into this area. The regular trail is way out of the way and too dangerous. Those two ladies spent three days up here, scouting out and putting natural rock markers in all the right places. With the amount of white quartz in the area, it was a perfect choice against the gray granite. Simply one small piece placed on large rocks at strategic places was all that was necessary. That was at least ten years ago, and you'll see those rocks are still there.

"We're going to turn off the Meadow Brook Trail and go due east and pick up the other Forest Service trail to finish the last leg into Bench. The regular trail is so bad, the US Forest Service estimated it would cost over a million dollars to get it into shape. This route is far more beautiful and safer, has minimal to no impact on the environment, and takes about an hour off the travel time. I got this route approved as a User Trail by the Forest Service, and I feel it should be the main route.

Trail Duck Markers

"You will see indications this was an established route back with the sheep outfits. They liked to stay high up on the ridges and out of the narrow river gorges. That makes perfect sense for you never know what to expect from year to year. Up here, the snow leaves first, getting warmed up by the radiant heat from the sun heating up the rocks underneath. Down low, in the gorges, it's usually shady and cooler since there's less time during the day for direct sunlight. It is also easier to cross the creeks high up at their starting point than down lower where the volume is greater. Yep, the old-timers were mountain wise. I'm sure many times they learned from the Indians. I know I would have asked."

After crossing an open granite mountainside with knockout views for about a mile, the group crossed Fall Creek. Letting the horses drink, Clyde started in again. "Pablo, I remember a few years ago, during the Rough Spur fire, this place was totally socked in with smoke. That fire burned about 150,000 acres and lasted over two months. During that time a large hiking trip was in this area. There was virtually no risk from the fire itself since the fire was quite a ways to the south. Just the smoke made it miserable when the wind blew in this direction.

"This group had a base camp over at Horsehead Lake, the same place where we are going today. During a day trip, one of the female members was up on top of Blackcap peak up there, with one of the group leaders admiring Guest Lake below them. I later heard the male leader made some remark about going skinny-dipping in the lake below. Well, apparently, this really pissed off the lady. She stomped off across the ridge and disappeared in the smoke. Nowhere could she be found the remainder of the day, and so the group leader had to call out on a satellite phone to start a Search and Rescue, or SAR for short.

"With so much smoke, the helicopters couldn't be used since visibility was so limited and thus too dangerous. More than forty Fresno County sheriff officers hiked this area in a grid fashion for several days and not a trace was found. I had a feeling that if this lady was still alive, she would most likely be along the exit stream out of the canyon. That's this one here, Fall Creek. The Sheriff's Office wanted to stick to the grid pattern type of search and I get that. That method has the highest success rate statistically.

"Nine days later they did find her, still alive. She had two broken legs and had crawled to Fall Creek at the point it joins with the exit stream from Horsehead Lake, where base camp was. I heard later, after leaving Blackcap Peak, she had returned to base camp, and even though it was dark, she decided to keep on hiking for some reason, most likely still mad.

"Well, she walked right out on that cliff over there and went over the edge. She didn't stop until reaching the bottom and had two broken legs from the impact. It's a miracle she wasn't killed right then. Later, she apologized publicly for making the poor choice to wander off alone, in the dark, in unfamiliar territory. I still feel that group leader owes her and the sheriff's SAR team an apology too. So, Pablo, this is another example of how poor choices eventually always lead to poor outcomes."

After getting back on the main Forest Service trail, the group continued up the canyon, following Fall Creek. This is where the string overcame the hikers of the group. All were doing well and were glad to see the senior members making it this far without mishap.

Pablo noticed they were getting closer and closer to a sheer cliff. About forty-five minutes up the trail, Clyde stopped the whole string and said, "This part you fellows get to walk up. With its steep switchbacks and drop-offs, it's far too dangerous for you to ride up. When you get started, you'll see why. At the top is McGuire Lake, the first of a chain of lakes that go along this plateau. That's where Bench Valley got its name. You hikers need to give us about a fifteen-minute head start. Otherwise, you will be too close and the horses might kick rocks down on you. Not so fast, Pablo, you're riding up with Deb and me."

Pablo looked straight up and felt his throat getting dry. After taking the bridles off the client riding horses and tying them to the saddle horns, Clyde started up the cliff trail. Past the first turn, Clyde halted, got off, and unsnapped the lead lines on each pack-horse past the first one. Clyde got back on his horse, and the group proceeded up the switchbacks. The loose horses stayed right behind each other going up the trail. Numerous times different horses had to double-step or pause to evaluate footing before proceeding. Pablo noted this would have been a serious problem if they had all been tied together. The only horse with the lead line still attached was the one Clyde was pulling.

Several times going up, the horses were on three levels of switchbacks at the same time. Pablo would look up and see horses' hooves at eye level, and looking down the straight cliff, he knew if the upper horse fell on him, his days were over. He silently mumbled he hoped his divine maker didn't pick this day to call him. Up they went. Sometimes the horses lunged and jumped up high rock steps and clawed their way up. A flatland or out-of-shape horse

Down a Cliff Trail

wouldn't have a chance here. Finally, the group topped out and McGuire Lake jumped into full view. Clyde hopped off and went down the pack string, snapping the lead ropes back on. None of the horses moved a muscle; they just enjoyed the rest. Clyde motioned for all to relax since it would be a good twenty minutes before the riders caught up. The group hikers were far behind.

Sitting down in the mountain heather, Pablo had a chance to finally settle his nerves. Clyde noticed this and remarked, "Heard your mumbling back there. Every so often these obstacles are placed in your trail of life. It's God's way of making sure you still believe in him."

Pablo was momentarily embarrassed but quickly realized Clyde was probably right. He was glad Clyde didn't elaborate but just motioned toward the saddle horses and said, "Let's get the bridles back on. The riders will be here soon."

Up came the three riders, one at a time, huffing but doing well. The leader said, "I sure understand why you insisted we walk up," the leader said. "Holy crap, if we had gone off that edge, it would have been real ugly."

"Yeah, not only that, my horse might have gotten a scratch," Clyde said. "Wouldn't want that now, would we."

The leader sat down on a nearby log, breathing hard and chuckling to himself. Soon, the three riders were back on their horses and heading up the trail. Clyde called back that they had only about thirty to forty-five minutes left before Horsehead Lake. Pablo heard the clients say the walk up was good to stretch the legs but they were glad to be riding again. Going by Guest Lake, Pablo recalled what Clyde had said about the missing hiker. Looking straight up, he could see Blackcap Peak. It was a good thing she didn't step off that cliff. It would have been a five-hundred-foot drop straight into the lake.

The group went by Colt Lake, then finally topped out and looked down on their destination, Horsehead Lake. Pablo could clearly see how this lake got its name. It was definitely shaped like a horse's head. Clyde had told him some Fish and Game folks, Dill and Criqui, gave the lake its name while on a pack trip back in 1948.

The string went around the lake to the opposite side and up in some rocks and trees. This would give the group some shelter if it got windy, plus it kept them away from most of the mosquitoes. About halfway through the unloading, the last of the group's hikers showed up. Thus all had arrived safe and sound.

With the last of the packhorses unloaded and the empty string put together, good-byes were said and Clyde led the trio back down the trail. Overnight camp was to be behind McGuire Lake. This was a winter avalanche zone he had found. Clyde said he liked this spot for several reasons. "First, it's away from the group so they won't be bothered by the night bells on the horses. Second, it's away from any lake. Never like to have any impact on lakeshore riparian zones. Third, it's a boxed-in area with cliffs on two sides. Our camp will be placed so the animals have to go right through us to escape, but that's not going to happen. Fourth, the moon comes right across the cliff tops from one end to the other. It's an evening view Deb and I just love. You'll see for yourself."

Sitting next to a small evening fire, Pablo could hear the soft chime of the horses' bells echoing off the cliff walls. Looking through the trees, he counted them. Yep, all twelve were contentedly eating as a group. When the sun finally went down, it didn't take long for the moon to pop up over the cliff on the left side of camp. He knew it would travel across the cliff top to the right before the sun came up again.

After Deb and Clyde went to bed, Pablo stayed up a little longer than usual this night. He just didn't want to miss any of the show the sky was displaying. Sleep was slowly overtaking him so he decided crawling into his sleeping bag and looking up through his tent netting would still be good. Lying down and viewing the moon, he vowed to stay up and not miss a thing. By the count of five, he was fast asleep.

The next morning, Pablo was awakened by Clyde delivering morning coffee to Deb still coiled up in her sleeping bag. The aroma never failed to open her eyes. As the camp trees came into view through Pablo's sleepy eyes, he could hear the horses' bells. Clyde said to Pablo, "That's sweet morning music to a packer. The horses are close, full, rested, and ready for the day's work. No need to rush this morning, since we're going out empty. Get some coffee and don't forget to pet Patsy and Dinkey. Let 'em stretch first. Was a long day for them yesterday too."

Soon, Clyde, Deb, and Pablo were bustling about getting camp packed up and horses caught, saddled, and loaded. Within an hour and a half, the trio was heading back down the trail. When they came to the switchbacks, Clyde kept the group tied together and proceeded down slowly.

Clyde called back, explaining, "Going down is much easier than going up, as long as you go slow. Let each horse have a chance to get the slack out of the lead line before moving farther. You need to have a good lead horse. One that understands light rein touches and is OK with a slow, slow walk. Many flatland horses don't understand this and just want to charge on. That's a big problem and gets worse in situations like this. Taking your time is always best and most of the time is faster. You'll find that is true with a lot of things in life. Slow down and get the job done right. The outcomes are always better. Step by step and don't worry, you'll get there."

CHAPTER 8

Tehipite

"Wake up Pablo. If ya hurry, maybe you can beat the sun this morning," Clyde called from over by the corral. Pablo could see the bunkhouse window was open and realized Clyde knew it too. That's why hollering was easier than walking over.

"Where we headed today?" Pablo asked after shuffling up to the hitching rail.

"Going to a place called Tehipite Valley. We first go through the John Muir Wilderness out of Wishon Lake and then on into Kings Canyon National Park. Tehipite is what the local Native Americans called the high rock overlooking the place. I think the name has a beautiful ring to it. Frank Dusy was the first white man to discover it back in 1869. Took the first photo ten years later. The top of the dome is 7,700 feet high and overlooks the whole valley below. The Tehipite Valley floor is only 4,500 feet. I've been on the top looking down, all 3,200 feet to the valley floor with the Middle Fork of the Kings River flowing through. Either direction, top down or bottom up, it's a sight that will knock your eyes out. Some people call the place Little Yosemite. Definitely a hidden gem but a pain in the butt to get into and out of.

"I hear, way back, the local Indians spent the winters there. How they were able to find the necessary resources to live comfortably is amazing. For all the centuries they occupied this area, there's virtually no footprint visible. Only a couple of painted rocks and grind holes. Talk about a minimal-impact existence, those folks had a lot to teach us, if we would only listen.

"Anyway, we will need four saddle horses for the riders and three for us. Deb's going too. She'll take them to the rim, which is about five hours' riding time in. There, the riders get off and walk the remaining distance down the steep switchbacks. You'll see why when we get there. Deb will return with the empty saddle horses and be back here by evening. We will continue on down to the bottom, spend the night, and head out early in the morning. We will need three packhorses for their gear and one for ours."

They pulled out Jay for Pablo and Harley for Clyde and caught up Camp for Deb. After they led out the horses and tied them to the hitching rail, Clyde and Pablo caught up the four clients' saddle horses. Since yesterday was a short ride and after today those saddle horses will get almost a week off, Clyde said it would be OK to take Howdy, Lupin, Cloud, and Jigger again. Pablo knew they would be coming back out with Deb. Next, Clyde directed Pablo to lead out the packhorses, Nosebag, Loper, Diamond X, and Poco. "We're taking only the A team down to Tehipite," said Clyde. "You'll find out why when we get on the switchbacks. All the back loads will be low, with all the weight at the bottom of the bags. Absolutely no top loads. Yeah, Pablo, this trip will show you the extremes of packing in the wilderness."

Clyde could see Pablo had a nervous look in his eyes. "Don't worry," Clyde commented. "Most likely you'll survive." As he walked away, straight-faced, toward the saddle room, he added, "By the way, ya did say your prayers this morning, didn't ya?"

He returned with a saddle in each hand and placed each saddle behind the assigned horse. Pablo, after finishing grooming their backs, began putting on the saddle pads and saddling. Clyde knew which saddles to get after looking at the clients. He usually let Deb do the finish adjustments during the orientation at the trailhead. After the clients' gear was on the loading dock, Clyde started packing the loads into the panniers. With all eleven animals saddled, the duo took a break when Deb hollered out, "Frying the eggs."

After the usual hardy breakfast and with lunch burritos in their pockets, Pablo and Clyde returned to the hitching rails and started loading up. Six horses went into Clyde's trailer and the other five into Deb's. After loading the eight pack bags, riders and horses were ready to go. Clyde told Pablo, "Both dogs have to stay here today, since we're going into the national park. No dogs allowed."

Both gooseneck trailer rigs soon pulled out, followed by the clients in their SUV, 7:00 a.m. sharp. Along the way, Clyde pointed out a huge mountain to the southeast. "That's Spanish Mountain. Was said the Spanish had a mine there. Everyone now figures that was a bunch of BS. Named by Silas Bennet, a pioneer back in the 1870s. Top of that mountain is a little over 10,000 feet. All the water drainage from here goes down the Kings River to Pine Flat Lake."

With the short drive to the trailhead, which included going over Wishon Dam, Pablo got another view of the eastern Sierra granite peaks outlined by the glow of the morning sun shining on their backsides. This sight always captivated him until it was lost in the approaching pine trees. After they unloaded and packed up the horses, everyone was ready to start out. Clyde always said it should take only fifteen minutes per pack load. Sure enough, Pablo noted after looking at his watch, it took an hour to finish the pack loads.

They headed up the trail, Deb in the lead followed by the clients, then Pablo leading the three packhorses loaded with the clients' gear, and Clyde in the rear pulling the single packhorse full of the overnight equipment for both of them. Pablo noted the hobbles around the necks of all the packhorses and both of their saddle horses. The necks of the other horses were bare since they were coming out this afternoon. Pablo remembered Clyde putting in the shoeing bag and bells for the packhorse he was pulling.

Soon Clyde called up to Pablo, "Keep an eye on each rider in front of you. From behind them it's much easier to make sure they sit up straight, keeping the saddle centered and their feet in the

stirrups. Ya help Deb out a lot by doing that. If anybody starts leaning to the left or the right, call out and we'll all stop and check the
cinch. We're going to do just that in about fifteen minutes, but we
must always keep a watchful eye out for any trouble."

After about ten minutes, the silence was broken when Clyde
started in again. "I remember, must have been over twenty-five
years ago, I took a guy named Charles Haid and his three young
children. He was a guy who starred in the TV series *Hill Street
Blues*. This was way before your time. I was taking them into the
Dinkey Lakes area.

"Everything was going along just fine when I heard him say
from behind, 'Hey, Doc! I think something isn't right here.' I turned
in the saddle and almost peed my pants. His saddle had slipped
to the left and there he was, sideways on the horse, still sitting on
the saddle and hanging on to the horn for dear life. I slammed
on the brakes, jumped off my saddle horse, leaving him ground
tied, ran back, grabbed Charles, and pulled 'im off. That saddle
horse of his—remember the name was Buffy—just stood still like
a statue and never moved. After I got them all to their chosen lake
and unloaded, I quietly walked over to Buffy and gave her a kiss.
Nobody saw it, 'cause I didn't want to embarrass the horse. Anyway,
the point is, even if you take all the precautions, ya never know.
That's why you must always keep a watchful eye on everything
when it comes to horses and people in the wilderness."

After crossing Rancheria Creek, where all the horses got
a drink, they soon came upon a pleasant meadow with a granite
dome as a backdrop. Clyde called to Pablo and the clients, "Notice
that rock cap on top of the mountain. That's Crown Rock. Top is
about 9,300 feet. Named also by Frank Dusy back in about 1870.
It can be used as a reference point since it is obvious for at least five
miles in most directions.

"Coming up soon we'll go through Crown Valley. This happens to be a private land inholding within the John Muir Wilderness. A family named Johnson owns it. I was told it was bought

Sign for Crown Valley and Kings Canyon National Park

off the courthouse steps back in the 1920s. I think this parcel is about eighty acres, and they have four other forty-acre parcels scattered around the area. I was shown the contract from back then. It included all this land, plus about six hundred head of cattle. At the bottom it read all for $1,000. I heard the old man Johnson came up here with his sons, who were in their early teens, dropped 'em off, and left. Telling 'em to go gather all the cattle and good luck. Well, that was a huge undertaking for those young kids, being in a totally unfamiliar area and somewhat green themselves. They nevertheless attacked the challenge. After all the cattle were gathered in, there were over nine hundred head. Quite a windfall.

"Anyway, this place has been in continuous family hands ever since. They don't run cattle here anymore, just use these log cabins for family vacations. Look straight ahead and up. You'll see another rock spire. That's Kettle Dome. Also first named by Frank Dusy back in the 1870s. You're getting the idea that Frank Dusy sure got around. Most important, he carried a camera and used it. Back then it took a whole packhorse just for the camera and equipment. Ya had to be dedicated."

Turning right at Crown Valley, then shortly taking a turn to the left, the group started the straight shot past the park boundary, then on to the rim. Getting close to the rim, Clyde called out to stop and let the packhorses get in front, saying it was too danger-ous to switch the horses' order while on the rim itself. Deb would ride in the rear, since the clients were following the last packhorse. That done, Pablo continued, only this time he was following Clyde. Approaching the rim, Pablo could hear a roar, coming from either the river or the wind, he couldn't tell which. Just then, a huge granite canyon opened up and Pablo couldn't see the bottom. He thought for sure he was going off into the open sky and into oblivion. At the last second Clyde turned in his saddle and called out to stop. Pablo still couldn't see the bottom.

"This is it, boys," Clyde said. "Just stay still, and we'll help each of you off, one at a time. Don't anybody move."

From the clients' body language and the scared looks on their faces, Pablo could see there wasn't going to be any argument. Immediately after dismounting, Clyde reached up, removed the hobble from his saddle horse, and applied it to the two front legs. This put the whole string in park. Getting each rider off took some time, as the horse had to sidestep uphill just a little to allow a flat place for the rider to land after dismounting. Otherwise, he would have fallen off the side and into the abyss. After the clients had dismounted, each empty saddle horse was turned 180 degrees, in place, and tied together in reverse order for the trip home. Being in the back before, Deb then became the leader. She led her string a short distance and tied them up so they could rest. The remaining animals in the string never moved a muscle. Not nervous at all, just enjoying the rest.

Clyde then motioned for the clients to come up to the rim, using hand signals because of the loud roar. Approaching the rim with the group, Pablo could finally see the bottom, clearly, straight down between both of his feet. Shock overtook him as he jumped back simply by reflex. Clyde chuckled and did a catwalk out to a rock outcropping, motioning for Pablo and the others to follow. Clyde pointed down to a brass disk in the rock and asked Pablo, "Recognize this?" Pablo nodded, seeing another benchmark. "Look close and what else do you see?"

Pablo got down on his hands. The letters J.R.H. 1951 came clearly into view. Clyde continued, "Yeah, Ray Hedgpeth put this here on the same trip as Post Corral. To help understand time, I was a year old when he placed this disc here. That would make it almost seventy years ago. Back that up, at most, only another hundred years and the Indians were the only humans around these parts. Helps put things in better perspective."

Clyde gathered the clients and said, "Pablo and I will head down first with the packhorses. Reason is, so we don't kick rocks down on you if you were ahead of us. There are over seventy-three switchbacks on the way down. We'll drop 2,500 feet in less than two hours. There's not a drop of water all the way down until you get to that river you see. That's why I had you fill your bottles back up the trail. It's about 2:00 so you will make it down to camp in plenty of time. No need to rush. Take your time and watch your step. Remember, this place is loaded with rattlesnakes and poison oak, so be careful where you place your hands. Put the slowest walker in front, the leader stays in the back. We will try to stop the pack string from time to time and let you guys catch up, but don't count on it. For the animals, going down is mostly a controlled slide. See ya on the other side." Clyde dove off the edge and disappeared. Pablo followed, convinced this was going to be the end of his short life.

After about eight switchbacks, Clyde stopped at the first flat place in the trail. He got off and went back down the pack string to each lead line snap, undid it, then secured it to the spider ring on the packsaddle of the horse in front. After the horses were freed, Clyde remounted and resumed leading the first packhorse only. Pablo followed all four, amazed that the string continued on as if still tied together. As they came around the next switchback, Clyde was then able to call up to Pablo, since he was just above him, "With 'em not being tied together, they're able to pay attention to their feet placement and not be pulled by the horse in front. Letting them go at their own pace is the safest way to travel the rough stuff. I call it loose leading. They've been raised since babies to follow the animal in front, and it is just natural to do so now. It's a herding instinct we're taking advantage of since they've lived their entire lives together. The last thing they want is to be left behind. Also, with all their pack string training they have no interest in passing each other or falling behind. If one stumbles and has to scramble to recover, no problem, since he's not being pulled from the horse in front. That's when big problems occur. This way, we avoid all that fuss."

After a couple more switchbacks, Clyde continued, "I've been told that from the top of Spanish Mountain up behind us, down to the bottom of the river gorge toward Pine Flat Lake, this area is deeper than the Grand Canyon. Yep, they say this is the deepest gorge in the continental US. That trail going down to the bottom of the Grand Canyon is a highway compared to this. Most of this trail is no more than ten inches wide and full of loose rock. Gets worse toward the bottom too. There used to be a small mine down here. The guy hauled out the ore on pack animals. They were tough back then, or maybe just desperate. I hear this was an old Indian trail at first. As you can see, it hasn't improved much."

As they continued to descend, Pablo started to get comfortable having to lie back on his saddle, almost on his horse's butt, and with both feet sticking straight forward. Clyde, seeing this, remarked, "Now you see why I make the clients walk. Too dangerous otherwise. If you went off here, it would be tough trying to get yourself stopped on this almost 70-degree pitch. I explained it to the leader when he booked the trip and he was OK with it. Think about it, they know they have to walk back up too. Told 'em, on the way back, they had to hit the trail at 5:00 a.m., while it's still dark. Otherwise, when the sun hits the side of the mountain where the trail is, the temperature jumps big time. If they waited until midday to start up, the one or two water bottles with 'em would soon run out and the group would find themselves in big trouble. Down in the middle of this canyon, the breeze doesn't get moving until late afternoon. So, until then, this whole canyon is an oven.

"Just staying on the trail sometimes can be a challenge for hikers. There was a gal several years ago who got off the trail and got lost. If you get ten feet off this trail and realize your mistake, the best action is to simply retrace your steps. So many people try to outguess their situation and take shortcuts. That, almost always, is a bad idea. Somehow she found a crack in the rocks with enough water to get by. She was out about a week before being found. I understand she wrote a small book on her experience. That lady's lucky to be alive."

As they continued down into the gorge, Pablo was shocked to see yucca plants. He hadn't seen them since he was a child in Mexico. Getting lower, they came upon a grove of what looked like bay leaf trees. He noticed Clyde reaching up and stripping leaves off the branches as he went past, never slowing his horse down. He then deposited some into the front zipper pouch of his overalls.

"Pablo, I'll put these in a small plastic bag later to take them back out to Deb. Makes spaghetti and roasts taste great. I don't think this is a bay but more of a California laurel. Seems these trees here pack a big punch. That makes this small bunch worth the haul out."

Continuing down further switchbacks, many times Pablo held his breath as Jay carefully stepped over rocks blocking the trail. With only inches to spare there was no room for error. He couldn't even swallow hard he was so scared. Jay got him past all these problem spots without even flinching. He just kept following the packhorse in front of his nose. Pablo looked down and was temporarily embarrassed, noting the whiteness on his knuckles from the tight grip on the saddle horn. He immediately told himself to relax, Jay would get him through this. He remembered what Clyde had said the other day: "The last thing these mountain horses want to do is fall. They will do most anything to avoid that waste of energy or possible injury. It's a survival instinct they are born with and never lose."

Down and down they went. Pablo wondered if this hole had a bottom after all. The only way he could see blue sky was to look straight up. Any glance from the right or left was met with sheer mountain wall. He had no idea how the Indians ever found this route to begin with. Pablo's respect for the Native Americans just kept growing. The only other way down would have been with a parachute.

Finally, the duo popped out at the bottom, to be met with the sight and roar of the Middle Fork of the Kings River. Seeing there was absolutely no chance they would be able to cross, Pablo was relieved when the trail turned left to parallel the river upstream.

Clyde called back, "Off to the right is where the old miner's cabin was. The heavy winter of 1996–97 created the flooding that took the cabin out. Nothing much left now, except downstream you can still see the round grinding-stone structure he built to crush the ore. I hear the mine site is downstream and up the side of that granite cliff area. I've never explored it. Tried once, but there was so much poison oak I decided to rethink the venture.

"We're coming up to the flat part of the valley where this group's going to camp. They will be right up close to the base of Tehipite Dome, next to where Crown Creek dumps into the river. At that juncture, I call it the Fish Store. Seems every time I or anyone else drops a line in, a trout hits it. Some are quite large for this country. You can catch so many you'll get tired of fishing. At that point, when ya put your pole down and relax, the scenery jumps out at you. Only then can you truly appreciate this place. The wonder of it grows on you, especially the awesome sight of Tehipite Dome shooting straight up 3,200 feet right over your head.

"Back through those oak trees, up against the base of the cliff, is a small cave formed by accident from the exfoliated granite coming off the mountain over the centuries. Not much room in it, but it would be better than nothing in a storm. We're going to unload over there, since it is reasonably close to water and has a commanding view of the dome. Also, the spot is somewhat open, so you can take advantage of the afternoon and evening breezes. Helps cool things down and keeps the bugs off ya."

Unloading the clients' three pack animals went fast. Just as the last pannier bag was emptied, the client group of four came up to camp. Pablo was glad to see that they were together and doing OK.

"Gentlemen, five days from now when I return, we'll do the same thing in reverse," Clyde said. "I'll be down here the evening before and camp. Ya need to get all packed up the night before so there will be much less fuss in the morning and you guys can head out before sunup. Remember, there's not a drop of water on the trail up, and ya don't want that sun catching you on the hillside. I'll then load up your gear and head up the trail to catch you. When you get to the rim, Deb will be there with the saddle horses. She will be coming in empty a day after me, to meet you, turn around, and head back. Pablo, we're going to mosey over that way about a hundred yards for our camp. Need to give 'em their space."

With the packers' gear unloaded, Clyde and Pablo started unsaddling all the horses, remembering to place the packsaddles in the same order as the string. With hobbles on and two of them with bells, the horses were turned loose to graze. The sun was setting up the side of Tehipite Dome while the two were setting up their tents. Over the small one-burner stove, Clyde heated up the usual canned dinner. Ravioli for Clyde and spaghetti for Pablo, along with lima beans and prebuttered bread that Deb had already wrapped in foil. In less than ten minutes, they were eating and sitting back, enjoying the light show up the rock face while the gentle evening breeze kept them cool.

After dinner, Clyde started heating up the stove for the coffeepot, not for coffee but for a bucket bath. He filled a collapsible bucket full of water, dipped the coffeepot into the bucket to fill it up, and then placed the coffeepot on the one-burner stove. After a boil was reached, the coffeepot of hot water was poured back into the bucket with the remaining cool water. Then the process was repeated two or three more times. Usually just the second time was enough to get all the water hot enough for a bath.

To set up a place for the bucket bath, Clyde would take a canvas pack tarp, the full water bucket, and the empty coffeepot out a ways from camp, usually behind some trees and far enough away from the river. Clyde returned and said, "Pablo, you first. When you're done, refill the water bucket and bring it back with the pot. Then I'll start the process over for my bath."

Pablo was always surprised how well this worked. The first coffeepot of hot water was just enough to get him fully wet after pouring it over his head while standing on the clean tarp. He then lathered up and poured the second pot back over his head. This got rid of most of the soap, but it usually took a third pot to finish the job, and the fourth to feel just great. The dirt and sweat off him, Pablo put on clean clothes and returned to camp with the water bucket full of stream water for Clyde's next bath.

Bath time over, both retired to their tents. Seldom did either see the need to stay up after dark, since every day was long and hard. Looking out through the netted tent roof, both could see the last of the evening light top out over the dome. The roar of the river and the moan of the evening breeze were all that could be heard. Sleep was immediate.

About midnight, Pablo was awakened by a very distinctive sound of crunching off in the oak trees. Not sure of the origin, he called over to Clyde, "What the heck is that? Sounds like a bear chewing on a bone."

Clyde chuckled and said, "Guess again, Pablo."

After some thought, Pablo tried again, "Could it be rocks falling down the cliff or rolling under the water in the riverbed?"

"Naw. Did ya notice the grass is mighty sparse down here. But the ground is full of acorns. Horses are picking 'em up and eating 'em. They hold a lot of food value. Down in the foothills, the cattle will feast on 'em too. You'll see. In the morning the horses' bellies will be full and none the worse for wear. Since they grow up having acorns around, these mountain horses know how much to eat and when to stop so as not to be harmed. Wouldn't want to keep them here for a month, but one night won't hurt them one bit.

"Speaking of bears, this place has more than its share. I remember a few years ago, I came down to haul a group out. As I rode by that evening I could see they had ropes with pots and pans hanging strung all around camp. It was clear they were having a bear problem.

"The next morning, the group was more than eager to head out. While I was packing up the camp, I noticed all the horses looking in the same direction over there. I stopped what I was doing and sure enough, there was a yearling bear approaching as if he owned the place. I reached down and took hold of a five-foot-long branch and started running directly at that young black bear. We got to within thirty feet of each other, when he stopped and stood up on his hind legs. I then picked up the pace running directly at him, hollering and waving this large branch. He dropped on all fours, reversed, and bolted to the brush pile he came from.

"I then walked back to the camp and continued loading the gear. Within five minutes, he came back out. I wasn't worried about him attacking the horses, but that bear sure made every animal in the string nervous. Makes it hard and dangerous to get the loads on 'em. Their whole attention is on the bear and not on me. Anyway, I picked up the same branch and ran full speed toward him again. This time he didn't turn until I was within ten feet. That's when I flung the large branch at 'im and it smacked his rear just perfect.

Allen with Bear

That part was pure luck. He then kicked it into high gear and ran back to the same brush pile.

"With all back to normal, I finished loading, keeping an eye out for him. That bear kept me entertained, though. He spent the whole time peeking around that brush pile, watching me. That part never seemed to bother the horses. I got loaded up as quick as I could and headed out. Didn't want to push my luck. Now, go back to sleep."

Way before daylight, Clyde was on his way out of camp to retrieve the hobbled horses with all the lead ropes draped around his neck and hanging over both shoulders. Pablo rapidly caught up with him to help. Sure enough, the horses stood in a group under the large oak trees, burping, talking politics, and ready to go to work. Pablo snapped the lead rope on the first packhorse, then just draped the rope end over a branch, leaving the hobble on. Both of them then secured the remaining animals and tied them off to the lead horse, one at a time. Only after they were all strung up did Pablo reach down, remove the last hobble off the front horse, and slowly make his way back to camp with the string following.

After all were saddled and the empty pack bags loaded up, Clyde led the group past the still-sleeping clients to begin the trek home. The sun wasn't up yet, but a light glow was beginning to indicate that morning was on its way. Clyde started up the bottom switchbacks, but after three turns, he stopped and dismounted. He walked back to undo the lead rope snaps from the halters and secure them to the spider ring of the horse in front. He began with the second packhorse until all were done, same as he had done on the descent the day before.

Clyde then remounted and called back, "Pablo, lean forward, keep your feet back, ease off on the reins so the horse can have his head, and hang on. We're going to let the horses choose their pace all the way up. Stay centered so you can help your horse, so he doesn't have to fight your weight. If you panic, sit up and pull back on the reins, or you'll go over backward down the mountain. That'll definitely wreck your day and mine too. I'd have to stop, hike down, and pick up all the pieces of you to take back to your momma. All that would slow me up at least half a day. Would put me back home after dark and Deb's dinner would be cold. Do us both a favor and trust your horse. You'll soon see why I don't allow clients to ride back up this grade either. Let's go."

Because of all the loose shale in the trail, the ride up was much different from the ride down. Going down yesterday was mostly just a controlled slide. Going up was lunge, jump, and scramble. The fight was on, and Pablo felt his horse was ready, as were the others. Every four or five switchbacks, Clyde's horse would stop instinctively on a flat stretch in the trail so all the animals could get a breather while standing comfortably. Pablo noticed Clyde never touched his reins. After only two or three minutes, the horses were breathing at a normal rate. Without even a small kick from Clyde, his horse took a deep breath and started the ascent again. Clyde had the lead rope of the first packhorse, but the others followed along in obedient fashion. Even though none were tied, they never got out of line or dropped back. Just a steady march up the unbelievable grade out of the canyon.

About a third of the way up, Clyde called back, "Pablo, notice how we're not in any particular hurry. Like any journey in life, keep your eye on the end point and stay slow and steady. Always keep in mind, the fastest way to reach your destination is slowly. Remember, life is a marathon, not a sprint. By the yard it's hard, but by the inch it's a cinch."

Upward they continued the steady march. Pablo was sure glad they started out early. Almost to the top, they saw the sun pop out and immediately felt the temperature jump twenty degrees. Sweat was starting to pour out from under his hat. The horses were only then beginning to show some lather. Topping out at the rim, past the benchmark, Clyde stopped, dismounted, and instructed Pablo to do the same. "Let your horse rest without you on him" was Clyde's command.

While the horses were getting their wind back, Clyde slowly went down the line and reattached the lead rope snaps back onto the halters. After the horses had rested, Clyde remounted. Before starting out, he turned in his saddle and called back to Pablo, "Take a good look back, 'cause after one turn in the trail, all that view will disappear." Pablo did so, but he couldn't take his eyes away from the sight of the awesomely huge canyon. He remained fixated even as the string started moving and went around the corner and the view vanished in the trees.

CHAPTER 9

Blue Canyon

Pablo peeked one eye open, then the other. Yep, he was going to beat the sun up again today. He felt satisfaction with his inner clock awakening him on time rather than an alarm clock. Today had some morning clouds, but the weather report promised they would clear out and leave the day sunny. The Sierra Nevada in California are known for the best high-country weather, and he now understood why.

He walked to the corral with his morning cup of cowboy coffee in hand and asked Clyde what's on the schedule for today.

"Well," Clyde responded, "we're going to a new place for you. It's called Blue Canyon. There are many places with that name all over this country, but this one is in Kings Canyon National Park. We head out the same trail as the other trip to Tehipite Valley, but we do not turn south. Just keep going east out of the Sierra National Forest and into the park. Taking a family in consisting of mom, dad, and three children, ranging from twelve to sixteen years old. Dad is an emergency-room doctor from Bakersfield.

"Getting up to Tunemah Lake is on dad's bucket list. It's a beautiful 11,000-foot-high lake that will knock your eyes out. From there you look straight up and see Tunemah Peak at just under 12,000 feet. It's a three-day venture for us just to get there. A day to get to Blue Canyon itself, then half a day to get to Tunemah Lake. The last portion up to the lake is too steep for the family to ride, and they understand that part they have to walk. The other half of the day is to get back to Blue Canyon and the third day is for the final trip out. It's the same thing in reverse when we go get 'em in about ten days.

"So, we'll need five saddle horses, four packhorses (three for them and one for us), and our three riding horses. Go pull out Howdy, Jigger, Spice, Lupin, and Cloud for this family to ride. Get Jay, Chowchilla, and Little Shot for us and Diamond X, Pearl, Loper, and Poco for the packhorses."

Pablo knew all of the horses by name at this point. No guidance was needed in retrieving the animals. With the process going faster, Clyde was able to concentrate on the clients' pile of gear on the loading dock. He noted the group had packed well for a ten-day outing. No extras, just the essentials, and well organized. All their gear would load well on the three packhorses. The fourth packhorse was a gear load for the three guides during the three-day trek.

It was most important for the loads to be perfect. That meant all heavy stuff at the bottom of the pack bags and nothing tied on top. The going would be steep and dangerous, and the horses would need all the advantage they could get. As Clyde always said, "They don't need to be fighting a top load all the way. It's just heck on their backs and always wants to throw 'em off balance. These horses have to work almost every day all summer, and treating them kindly is not only the ethically correct thing to do but wise. There is never any room, or toleration, for abuse in this business."

Once the horses were saddled and the gear was in the flatbeds, loading the horses into the trailers was next. Both trailers, if full, could transport twenty at a time. Today only twelve were going, so six and six left plenty of room for each.

As they were pulling out, Clyde had to tell Patsy and Dinkey, "Sorry, no go on this trip. Heading into the park and cute dogs like you just aren't allowed. The two of you will have to settle for guarding the fort while we're gone. Are you both up for that?" The dogs returned to the porch and sat down, both wagging their tails. "I guess that answers that question," Clyde said.

Out the gate the whole procession went, heading toward the Rancheria trailhead, across the Wishon Lake dam.

After unloading at the trailhead, Deb got to fitting the saddles to the clients and delivering the usual orientation. All this took, at most, thirty minutes, and then up the trail Deb and the clients went. Getting the preloaded pack bags on the horses went quickly, and within forty-five minutes Pablo and Clyde were following. Clyde radioed up to Deb advising of their departure, and she called back on her location at that time. That way they knew where each other was.

At this elevation the forest was mostly full of red fir, some lodgepole pines, a few sierra cedars, and an occasional sugar pine. The trail had mild undulations but was basically flat going compared to other routes. Clyde and Pablo caught up to Deb and the clients, and the group passed the old Forest Service Guard Station log cabin and soon came upon Crown Valley. Pablo had been here before on the trip to Tehipite. This time the string didn't turn right toward the south. Instead, they continued straight heading east. Crossing Crown Creek was easy as it was less than two feet deep and no problem for the horses. Soon, the group passed the Kings Canyon National Park boundary and started up the steep Kettle Ridge.

As the group slowly ascended Kettle Ridge, Clyde chimed in. "Pablo, a few years ago, I hauled in a group of Canyoneers. That's a new term for a type of exploration-slash-mountain-climbing I had never heard of before. It so happens to be that nobody had ever explored the exit stream from Blue Canyon as it descends down to Tehipite Valley and joins with the Middle Fork of the Kings River at a place called Blue Canyon Falls. That's no mystery since that creek gorge is full of narrow, slick drop-offs and you had better be experienced with climbing gear, etcetera, or you could be trapped and out of luck. I dropped 'em off up ahead at the crossing, then headed back to Crown Valley and on down to Tehipite Valley to pick them up two days later. The whole group of eight made it, but boy were they beat. Seems they had to do some thirty different rappels, but all made it OK. They were sure stoked about the accomplishment. Then I had to pack out all that heavy climbing gear up and out of the hole called Tehipite. And Pablo, you know what I mean."

The slow climb gave Pablo time to pause and reflect. Apparently, Clyde did the same and chimed in. "Pablo, I don't think I told you much about the previous owner of the pack station named Bea Wright and her daughter, Stephanie. They got into this business by being the financial backer to a farrier who was supposed to run the place. That worked for about three years, then this horseshoer ran off with a lady and her three kids to Oklahoma. That left the Wrights holding the bag, and they had to step in and run the outfit.

"The daughter, Stephanie, was the real packer. She always rode horses but loved her pack mules. One year over in Bishop Mule Days she won the packing contest. Had to compete against all the men, and she whipped their butts. It was somewhere in the mid-1980s, long before the Me Too movement. Stephanie was one tough lady. We sometimes use the expression 'Has a lot of bark on her.' She had a genuine heart of gold, but I've seen people get on her bad side and the language she would use would make a sailor blush. Sure knew how to handle a pack string, though. Got lots of Stephanie stories; someday I'll let you in on some of 'em. Anyway, her mother, Bea, was just as tough but a gentle soul.

"My uncle, Auggie Wolf, introduced me to this business. I mentioned earlier, I started out as a backpacker, but he got me into using horses right after coming home from finishing my medical training. Bea always wanted to meet him but never did. I remember one of the first times I sat down and chatted with Bea. She pointed to a picture on the wall and proudly pointed out how beautiful the image was, with its long ears, perfectly shaped nose and shoulders. I stood up, walked over to the picture, stepped forward and back, trying to get a different focus, and tilted my head as dogs sometimes do. All I saw was a picture of the ugliest mule I had ever seen. Right then I knew this lady can find beauty in anything. I told that story when I spoke at her funeral. Also, I pointed out a fact I discovered when I walked up to the graveside service down at Academy cemetery. Even though she never got to meet my uncle Auggie, it so happened she was being buried right next to him. Yeah, bizarre but true."

As they went up the switchbacks on Kettle Ridge, Clyde continued, "Over to the right, cross country, is the backside of Tehipite Dome. The ridge joins up with the dome almost to the top. For climbers to approach from this side is much easier. They side-cliff-climb around, then rappel down to the valley floor, and climb back up after setting their pins and ropes. I understand nobody has been able to start from the bottom and go up. Too much rock exfoliation, which makes it dangerous for the lead climber and for those in line behind him. Getting hit in the head by a fifty-pound rock going full speed would not make your day. A helmet would not help a bit. I packed down one group who tried but aborted the attempt soon after starting.

"Anyway, a few years ago I took in a couple up this route and then off trail a short distance to a water source where they wanted to make camp. He was on a scouting trip for a future climbing outing on Tehipite. He had his fiancée with him, and she was an ER nurse with a lot of experience. The climber was a structural engineer. He worked on dams. He's the guy who would rappel down the side of a dam to do inspections. After getting all his needed information, he would climb back up, go back to the office, and do the calculations and plans for the construction crew to follow for doing the repair.

"This guy had climbed all over Europe and Argentina. He's one of those hard-core dudes. All the way in we talked about the various pickles hikers and climbers would get into and need rescuing. He went on and on about in Europe, you can't get a climbing permit without taking out rescue insurance. The helicopter was making numerous trips a day during the climbing season and all that costs money. These countries turned to rescue insurance as the answer to this budget-draining problem. It seems to be working since the program has been going on for many years now. He spent a lot of time elaborating on the inexcusable lack of experience of many climbers in this country. Upon reaching the spike camp location, I unloaded them and their gear, waved good-bye, and headed home.

"The next morning about 10:00 a.m., I got a satellite phone call from the fiancée saying her husband-to-be had gone out for a short reconnaissance walk the prior afternoon and didn't come back. Keeping a calm demeanor, she asked when would be a good time to flip the switch and call for a Search and Rescue. I told her to hold off a few hours. I had a plan and would be there ASAP.

"As Deb made me two hamburgers, thinking I was going to be out late, I went out and saddled Jigger. I then hauled over to the trailhead, unloaded, and started in. The trip in for them the day before was six hours one way, but I double-timed it in and arrived at their spike camp in three hours. It was 2:00 p.m. by then. I had brought an extra radio and put it on our channel so no one else would hear. She and I could talk back and forth. This way it eased her anxiety somewhat. I said we would give it two hours. By 4:00 p.m. if we had not found him, I would call in a SAR. This would allow enough daylight for the helicopter to do a decent search. It wasn't going to get dark until after 8:30 p.m. during that time of the summer.

"Off I went, taking a wide loop to attempt to cross his trail. I was coming close to Tehipite Dome and still hadn't crossed his trail yet but was done with only about half the intended loop. I looked across a canyon and noticed a spot that looked out of place at the rim of a sheer drop-off. I called out, and he answered in a desperate voice. I was able to verbally guide him laterally across the rim and over to a place where I could join him with my horse. I then radioed his fiancée and advised I had made contact, much to her relief. When the climber and I met up, I thought he was about to cry. Said after leaving camp, he didn't get his bearings for the return and just kept walking. He knew where he was, since you could plainly see

Tehipite Dome but simply had no clue where camp was. He had spent all afternoon walking in circles. He tried to settle down next to a log for the night, but after two hours got up and started out walking again in the dark. That is the dangerous part. Many have fallen off cliffs trying to do this. Sometimes they are found and sometimes not. He was totally wiped out by this time and knew if he had to spend another night out, most likely he would not survive, especially since he was right on the rim of a sheer cliff.

"Needless to say, he thought I was an angel from heaven, arriving with a horse to serve as a taxi and providing the best hamburger he had ever eaten. Up on the horse he went, and with me leading, off we went back to camp. I radioed to the fiancée and said we're on our way. I was able to take a beeline directly back to his camp in forty-five minutes. Upon arriving, I called out to his fiancée in somewhat of a smart-ass tone, 'Here he is whether you want 'im or not.' They rejoiced in the reunion, I tipped my hat and bid them farewell, and off I rode home. Got back after dark, but I was satisfied no SAR had to be called. We has saved the county taxpayers a lot of money and kept him out of the newspapers. I heard later she actually did marry him. I still admire the cool she maintained during the whole thing. No matter what happens in any ER she is working, I feel the patients are in good hands with her. Later in the summer, the whole group of about six climbers did come back and I packed 'em in and out of the backside of Tehipite Dome. They went down and up the east side, which I was told had never been done. Anyway, all ended up well."

Continuing up the west side of Kettle Ridge, Clyde said, "Kettle Dome, up ahead, was first named by Frank Dusy back in the 1870s. I have read he first called it Kettle Rock, but the name was changed probably by the US Geological Survey during the 1908 mapping survey. Most likely this ridge was named Kettle Ridge at that time too."

Pablo noticed, as usual, that all the clients were listening intently to Clyde's elaboration on the history of the country they were traveling through. He knew they were always glad to be included in the impromptu lectures that took place during the rides.

They soon topped out over Kettle Dome and headed down the east side of the ridge to the exit stream of Blue Canyon. Descending the switchbacks was easy for the stock, and soon the group was at the creek side and following the trail leading up to Blue Canyon itself. Clyde motioned to the group that this was the drop-off point for the Canyoneers group he had talked about before. Pablo understood why Clyde had mentioned the group earlier because here the creek was so loud you had to shout to be heard.

As they ascended, the creek noise lessened, and Clyde started in again. "Blue Canyon itself was used as a summer holding area for young replacement heifers of the Sample Cattle Company. We'll pass through a narrow place in the trail right up ahead. Here three narrow logs were placed across the trail to block the cattle from getting back down the trail. It's a perfect spot, since there are boulders and steep hill on both sides. This is the only way in from this direction.

"The other route is over Mountain Meadow, which is way up Kettle Ridge. That trail is steep, has brush two stories high, and is never used. When we get to the meadow itself, you'll see this is a perfectly isolated location to keep the animals here all summer with no worries. What's left of a small cabin is on the left just across the creek. I remember you could crawl inside, but now it's just a pile of decomposing logs, soon to melt back to nature. When the Kings Canyon National Park expanded its boundaries, this area was included, so the Samples had to leave. That marked the end of an era."

After dropping off the clients at one end of the meadow in the trees, the horse group moved to the other end and unsaddled. Deb, Clyde, and Pablo set up camp and hobbled out the horses to graze contentedly in the belly-deep grass. Pablo took a moment to look around and admire this beautiful valley. Talk about postcard material, this was it—steep cliffs and mountains on three sides and a narrow exit at the lower end. He could clearly see why this was a prized location for the early cattlemen. After dinner, Pablo climbed into the sleeping bag in his small tent and was soon rocked to sleep by the soft chime of the horses' bells.

Morning sunshine came late due to the narrowness of the canyon. Clyde was already up, had given Deb her morning coffee, and was out getting the horses in. Since they would not need the client riding horses, Clyde needed to bring in only about half of the string. That's why he went out alone and let Pablo get some extra sleep. The client riding horses were to get the day off, and Pablo could see there was no protest from them.

The saddling almost completed, the clients walked past waving, indicating their gear was ready to load up. Clyde called out, "We'll see you at the lake," and the group disappeared in the trees going up the steep hillside.

Clyde turned to Pablo and said, "Several years ago I spent a full day scouting a route up this side of the mountain. I had been told there was an old trail up, but I couldn't find it. That's a 45-degree pitch, and a trail route would be a huge benefit to the horses. If I could find it, I would be able to take advantage of all the scouting done by the early sheepmen, cattlemen, and Native Americans in this area. Having that knowledge would be most helpful.

"I had a patient named Jay Robinson and knew he had spent a lot of time here herding cattle in his youth. When he came in for his next appointment, I asked him. He was more than eager to explain. I knew he was in his early eighties, and it had been over sixty-five years since he was up here, so I wondered about the accuracy of his information. Nevertheless, I quietly listened.

"He explained that from the old cabin, look straight across the creek and you will see an old dead tree snag. Go directly to it and that's where the trail starts. Then follow the switchbacks up the mountainside. When you get to the top, you'll come to an old salt log we used. Continue on east and you will approach Alpine Creek. That's where you break left from the trail and follow upstream. The old trail will continue on to Simpson Meadow. The trail was so dangerous the National Park Service blew it up to prevent anyone from using it. Good thing, because parts of the trail were suspended on chains over the cliff. Keep going up Alpine Creek until it stops. There you will find a boulder field, and you will have to tie up your horses and walk the last hundred yards to Tunemah Lake.

"Well, the next time I came up here, I had a day layover and planned to scout it out on what I had thought was questionable information. I rode over to the remains of the cabin and looked in the direction for the log snag he had talked about, knowing full well what the small chances were it was still standing. I had to blink my eyes for there it was, but I thought, what are the chances this was the right snag. I then rode across the creek and up to the snag and to my shock there the trail was, hidden in the rocks but plain as day. Up I went following this remarkably preserved trail, thankful for the route my predecessors had chosen. Every time I stopped and looked back, I determined this was the only way possible up this mountain with loaded packhorses. At the top of that ridge, I suddenly slammed on the brakes for right in front of me was the old salt log Jay had talked about. At this point I was a full believer.

"Continuing on, I came up to Alpine Creek and turned left. I had to cross it only once as the conditions got steadily easier as I went up. As I approached the end of the tree line, the boulder field came into clear view. After tying up my horse and doing a short walk around, I found a small spring that was the start of Alpine Creek. The area had numerous flat spots, and I felt I had found a perfect place to put any future clients. Walking up the football field–length boulder field, I popped out and was looking down on the deep, clear blue water of Tunemah Lake. This lake is perched almost right on top of the mountain with no entrance stream. The exit stream is a four-foot-wide natural rock spillway with water gushing out and going almost north, not back down Alpine Creek, which was strange. Obviously the lake is fed from beneath with water under pressure geologically. You will see when we get there, the fish look like submarines the water is so clear.

"Anyway, I'm telling ya this history to remind you to always keep an open ear for any and all information you can get during your ride down the trail of life. You get information sometimes from sources you have the least faith in. Often this turns out to be the most valuable. Old Jay Robinson is gone now, but every time I'm in this area I think of him and get an appreciative smile on my face. Now let's go load up their gear and head up that mountain."

After loading up the clients' gear, Clyde and Pablo went back to their camp. Deb was ready to go with lunches made and camp secured. Up the mountainside they went. Starting from the old snag, the zigzag trail slowly took them up and up. Topping out at the ridgeline, Clyde pointed out the old salt log. It was near a small meadow that Clyde said he thought was called Grouse Meadow. A snow marker pole was there so it was used during the winter snow surveys. Onward to the east they traversed until arriving at Alpine Creek. Pablo could see the trail continue to the right, but the group turned to the left to head north up Alpine Creek. Mostly this area was slab granite and relatively easy traveling. Clyde pointed out a lake with no name to the left. He had placed the Eisele couple there several years ago, long before they had children. The lake is right up against a granite cliff and has a beauty all its own. No fish in it, though. Up they went, getting close to the tree line where the riders encountered the clients. Pablo was in awe of the physical tenacity of the three children. Clyde pointed this out and said, "See that, Pablo, maybe there is hope for the younger generation."

After unloading their gear and restringing the empty packhorses, Clyde motioned to Pablo to follow him up to the lake. "You've come this far, might as well see the lake for yourself." Off the two walked. Deb said she had already seen the lake several times and would stay and watch the stock.

Pablo stopped in his tracks at the first view of Tunemah Lake. Not a tree was in sight, and the rock had a distinct red tint. Feeling he was on the moon, he crept up to the shore and looked down.

Sure enough, he saw a huge trout down deep. It did remind him of a small submarine. Clyde chuckled and said, "It's just an illusion. The deep water will give a magnification that sometimes fools ya. But it's still a beautiful sight. I'll bet no more than eight or ten people happen by here each summer. This place has been untouched for eons. Before we leave, walk over and look at the spillway."

Pablo walked over to the place Clyde pointed out and, following the water exiting the lake, looked out over the cliff. He was amazed how the land below looked like the moon with craters. Only here the craters were full of water. The land in front of him was totally different from the land behind. He sat on the rock next to the spillway, mesmerized by the unique geology. After a longer time than he realized, Pablo turned to look back and noticed Clyde motioning for him to return. He then remembered the day was only half done. Deb was waiting, and there was still the ride back down the mountain.

Getting back on his horse, Pablo still couldn't get the dramatic image of Tunemah Lake out of his mind. He never considered there could be such beauty anywhere. He figured there would be some pretty areas in his native Mexico, but he had never seen them. Up here in the Sierra Nevada were sights he would never forget.

Once he was back in the saddle, Pablo asked Clyde where the name Tunemah came from. Clyde responded with a slight grin. "Well, I heard it came about back around 1878, when Frank Dusy and Bill Coolidge were herding sheep in this area. Their Chinese herders were having trouble getting the band to stay headed in the right direction. Remember, they had to go down the almost-cliff-like trail to Simpson Meadow. Anyway, over all the racket from the sheep, the dogs barking, all they could hear from the herders was 'teu-na-mah-ne, teu-na-mah-ne,' over and over. I don't understand the literal translation, but it makes derogatory reference about an act with somebody's mother or grandmother. Beyond that, I don't even want to know."

Down they went, switchback after switchback, until finally they reached the valley floor. After the short ride around to camp, the horses were unloaded, unsaddled, and hobbled out to graze. They joined the other saddle horses, which were already full from eating but seemed curious about the journey the others had taken that day. With all chores done two hours before sunset, Clyde suggested that Pablo hike up the trail toward the back of the valley. "Take a walk and look around, you can't get lost. If ya get off the trail, just follow the creek back down and you will bump right into camp. Go check out the five lakes up there, but just be back before sunset. I don't want to have to waste time tomorrow morning looking for ya," Clyde said with a smile.

Hiking up the trail, Pablo soon came upon a boulder slide zone that had come down the mountain and crossed the trail. Getting horses across this area would have been tricky for they would have had to get off and slowly walk each animal across one at a time. Up he went, noticing the trees were getting more sparse. The first small lake came into view. Pablo heard only the occasional chirp of the chickadees and pikas. Since it was evening and no fish were feeding on the lake surface, Pablo figured the lake was barren. Up he continued until arriving at the fifth and last of the lakes in the small chain. None of these had names, and Pablo felt he truly was in a forgotten corner of the world, inhabited only by the small critters who have called this place home for thousands of years. Absorbing the whole impact took more time than Pablo had expected. Startled to see the sunlight creeping up the canyon wall, he realized time was passing and he had to get back to camp. Back down the trail he went, in no particular hurry, just enjoying the total experience.

Crawling into his sleeping bag, full from dinner and gazing up at the stars through the screen netting of the tent roof, he determined today was the best day of the whole wilderness experience. He quietly chuckled, realizing he said that to himself every night.

The soft sound of the distant horse bells awakened Pablo at first light. With the first eye opened, he could see Clyde pouring the morning coffee. Yep, it was time to crawl out and start the day.

The duo had all twelve horses back in camp and ready to saddle in about thirty minutes. Deb had heated the ready-made burritos, and they all sat down for breakfast. Loading all the horses went slowly, since none were in a hurry to leave the beautiful surroundings of Blue Canyon. Looking up the side of the mountain they came down the previous day, Clyde pointed out a black bear munching on blueberries in the early-morning sun. It was too far away to be of any concern to the horses, so work continued at the relaxed pace. As they started to leave the campsite, Pablo did his usual survey and was always impressed with the way Clyde insisted on leaving the area as they had found it. The only visible signs they had camped there were foot- and hoofprints. Because of the natural litter of the forest floor, even these were barely noticeable. After one rain, they would be gone.

CHAPTER 10

Geraldine Lakes

Pablo was the first one up this morning, he thought, triumphantly stepping into the cookhouse, only to see Clyde handing him a cup of coffee, then sitting down next to his half-full cup.

"We're heading to a lake called Geraldine," said Clyde. "It actually is a trio of lakes. Has a lower and an upper and a third, seldom-seen lake between them but off the trail. Few people even know about that one. All three are unique in their own way. You'll know what I'm talking about when you see 'em. This is a large hiking group of fourteen. We are taking only their gear but will need about nine packhorses to get it all in. They will be staying a week, so we will probably get by with eight for the return trip. Look out the window. That pile of stuff is our chore for today. The group has already headed out. Took off just before daybreak. We'll meet up at the lower lake. Refill your cup and let's get to work. I'll be out there after I take Deb hers."

Pablo was overwhelmed when he got close to the huge pile. He figured it would take at least twenty packhorses, but Clyde had said nine, so that's what he would get gear for. It was always surprising to Pablo how Clyde could simply glance at a mountain of gear and determine exactly what the packhorse count would be. He had never seen him miscalculate. Out of the tack room he carried eighteen pack bags and piled them on the cart. It still took three trips over to the loading dock.

Clyde motioned for Pablo to start pulling out horses and begin saddling. No instructions were needed by now. Pablo knew which needed to go on this trip. He purposely chose the younger end of the string. The trip was relatively short, four hours in and the same out. The horses had been working hard so the older animals needed the rest more; they'd earned it. Pablo brought out Nevada, Pearl, Sundown, Loper, Poco, Diamond X, July, Cinch, and Tobacco, one at a time. All were strictly packhorses. No clients were riders on this trip so they didn't need a backup combination saddle and pack-horse today. Pablo then got his saddle horse, Jay, for today's ride. As he was leading out Jay, Clyde simply called out, "Harley." No other conversation was necessary. Pablo returned to the corral for the remaining horse needed for the day. He knew Harley could step out fast. With no clients to slow the group down, Pablo understood Clyde's choice. He wanted to hustle in and beat the group to the destination, unload, and head back before dark.

After all the horses were saddled and the gear was packed, it became obvious that two trucks and trailers were going to be necessary. Eleven horses can be carried in one gooseneck trailer, but they can't have saddles on them. Not enough room. Also, with all eighteen pack bags loaded, both flatbed trucks would be needed anyway. On the return, one could be used, since the bags would be empty and that would leave room for the horses' saddles. By figuring this math and physics problem out in advance, Deb would only have to help with the trailer in the morning. The two could get everything back in one rig that evening.

Out the gate the group went at 7:00 a.m. sharp, Dinkey and Patsy eagerly sticking their heads out the back of the flatbeds. With Deb's help, all nine packhorses were loaded up and strung together in thirty minutes. Pablo and Clyde lifted the loads on and Deb did the tarp and lash tying. The string was put together as the loading progressed. Before 8:00 a.m. the duo was ready to head up the trail. Clyde gave Deb a kiss and said he would call on the radio when they got close to the trailhead that evening. Deb and Clyde were still waving to each other as the last packhorse disappeared into the trees.

The first twenty minutes or so of any ride requires total focus on the string. Any tilting of loads must be fixed immediately. Making small adjustments to avoid problems is much faster and easier than the time and effort necessary after a big issue arises.

A furry animal scampering along a log to Pablo's right caught his eye. The foot-and-a-half-long animal stopped and so did Pablo. This halted the whole string, and it didn't take Clyde but a moment to notice the cause of the interruption.

"Take a good look, Pablo. What do you think it is?"

The animal stood still for what seemed an eternity before Pablo finally spoke up. "Looks like a fisher. Its ears are less than half the size of a martin. There is no orange color under his throat, and this animal is much larger than a martin. From what I've read and seen in pictures, I'd say this looks like a fisher. Only thing, you don't see fishers out in the day much. This one looks young, though. That might be the reason."

Clyde smiled. "You're catching on. I like your thought process. Keep it up."

After about an hour down the trail, Clyde called up to Pablo, "Do you notice anything different about this trail we're on now?"

Pablo surveyed the route and surroundings. He noticed the burn area on the right and no evidence of recent burning on the left but, other than that, nothing.

"You would never know that during the Rough Fire, a bulldozer went right up this trail to make a firebreak," Claude continued. "The US Forest Service fire crew then used this line to start a backfire to the right. It worked, and that is what kept the fire from blasting through all the miles of Wilderness Area to the left. After the fire was out, a hand crew came through and put all the natural material back on the route. Even curved the trail back and forth to create a natural appearance. After a couple of winters, you have to look really hard to notice any evidence a dozer was ever through here. You can only see an occasional scratch on a rock here and there.

"As for the 2015 Rough Fire itself, many lessons can be learned. Three different log-thinning projects were scheduled along the upper ridge way over to the right. Each was around four hundred to six hundred acres. During the 1990s the environmental groups blocked them from ever happening. In my opinion the Forest Service made a poor defense for the necessity of these three projects. It appeared it was about the logs, but nothing could be further from the truth. They were needed as fire defense zones. These are necessary to help contain natural fires from gaining momentum and getting catastrophic.

"For eons, nature has provided lightning strikes during all types of conditions. These include times during high-moisture periods, which prevent the fires from getting too large. They can be limited to a few acres out to several hundred. This is necessary because when a strike occurs during drought times, the fire is buffered by these naturally made defense zones. By repeating this over and over, the forest floor is much cleaner and healthier. The tree density should be about only seventy-five to a hundred trees to the acre. But look to the left, it must be well over five hundred. That's a time bomb just waiting to explode. The Forest Service has learned a lot in the past twenty years as far as clean logging goes. Now is the time for both sides to come together, make wise choices, and implement good practices that truly benefit the forest and all the people who rely on it. That includes most all of us, either directly or indirectly."

After about thirty minutes of quiet riding, Clyde started in again. "Pablo, thinking of that fire reminds me of the only Forest Service packer I respect. Her name is Deborah McDougald. She has spent her whole adult life around horses, mules, and the mountains. Upon getting her bachelor's of science degree in animal science from UC Davis, she worked as a commercial packer over in Cedar Grove in Kings Canyon National Park. After several

Debbie McDougald

seasons she started working for the US Forest Service as a government packer. Bringing many years of successful commercial experience to a government job is extremely valuable to the public. Deborah approaches issues with a viewpoint based on practical experience and not on a manual written by some desk jockey. She knows what the animals can and can't do in the high country. All the time she conducts her efforts in an environmentally friendly manner. To do this takes know-how and talent and can be learned only from decades of experience. It never ceases to amaze me how many people stop early in their learning process and never progress after that. You'll find that with all walks of life. When you choose to stop learning, the changing times and circumstances only lead to confusion and rebellion. Neither of which lead to progress."

Clyde took a breath but continued nevertheless. "Ms. McDougald and I do have our differences. She is fixated on the saintlike value of mules. You won't see her pack anything but a mule, even though I notice she is most always riding a horse. I get from her all the supposed virtues of mules over horses and I respond with the value of choosing all horses. She cites the longevity of mules, their ability to live by eating only pine needles, their sure-footedness, the hardness of their hooves, and their ability to go long distances with very little rest. I reply that these virtues are probably true. Then I start in with elaborating on the bright side of horses. This includes their ability to reproduce (all mules are sterile, so if they're so great, why didn't God just make 'em in the first place), their equal sure-footedness, and their hoof health if raised in the mountains. I also mention getting the right breeding selection that maximizes food intake conversion to maintain good body conditioning.

"The high cost of mules in today's market is due to the overabundance of mule enthusiasts. For example, for the cost of one riding mule, I could buy five horses in today's market. One of which would typically be an excellent horse, two would be fair and with work turn out good, one would be strictly a packhorse, and the fifth would be a junker I would get rid of. If horses are maintained in good health and conditioning, their live expectancy equals that of a mule. A good percent of my herd is well into their thirties and still working.

"As you have noticed, these horses can go all day in this altitude and not even break a sweat. All things considered, my choice of horses over mules is strictly a business decision. You still have to shoe mules the same as horses. That's because of the terrain the animals are forced to go over. Being on a forced march over granite all day long, day in and day out, requires steel on their hooves, no matter what. I guarantee an animal will get sore after only a few days up here without hoof protection. A few private horse people will come up here with flatland horses and think natural is best. I think that is pure foolishness. The horse is a plains animal. It evolved in that environment, where protection was not necessary. Up here in these rocks it's a different story.

"I did a test case once. I had a bunch of Bureau of Land Management horses I got through their adoption program. These animals were raised in the high-desert area of Nevada. Getting shoes on them was always a fight, but I always prevailed, except with one in particular. This mare would fight me to the death if I kept at it. We would go around and around for hours. Nothing but kicking and biting is the only outcome I got, and sooner or later one of us was going to get seriously hurt.

"Finally, I decided to try out a professed theory about their supposed hard hooves. Off we went for a two-day trip. When I got back, she definitely had sore feet. I couldn't use her for a month. After that I only took her out on one-day trips. Never did get shoes on her. Finally, I exercised the only option for a horse like that. Got her a new owner. During the winter all my horses, with their shoes removed, are kept on a one-thousand-acre portion of the ranch that is just a huge mountainside full of rocks. By just observing, I noticed the horses make paths around all the rock piles. Never over them. Given a choice the last thing they want is to get sore feet. Up here there is no choice. So, that is why shoes are a necessity."

After about twenty minutes of silence, allowing time for Clyde to catch his breath and Pablo's head to clear, Clyde continued. "Anyway, Pablo, Ms. McDougald is now acting wilderness manager of the Sierra Nevada John Muir Wilderness Area and is also the permit administrator for all the commercial pack stations in this forest. With all the hats she has to wear I have no idea how she gets anything done. Without her, this wilderness area would be in a world of hurt. Her heartfelt dedication has the respect of everyone, even though I tease her about her crazy mule infatuation."

Onward the group went. Approaching Crown Valley, Clyde motioned to the left and pointed out a small log cabin with a huge red fir tree that had crushed it dead center. "That was the original Forest Service ranger cabin. Really tight inside, but most of the cabins in those days were small. The heavy winter of 1996 took down a lot of trees, including the one that took out the cabin. The cabin was only a reminder, though. It had long been abandoned and replaced with the new one coming up on the right.

"I was shown a picture from a patient with her father standing upright inside the walls while he was building the cabin. It was dated August 1941. He was a seasonal ranger who apparently knew how to build a good log cabin. Think about it. That was only months before Pearl Harbor. In the picture of her grinning dad, the log walls were waist high to 'im at the time. That cabin has stayed upright and tight all these years. The Forest Service doesn't use it anymore and that's a shame."

The string turned right to head south and toward Geraldine Lakes. This required a climb up a ridge that led to a top-out portion with knockout views. Way off to the left Pablo could see Kettle Ridge, Kettle Dome, the Obelisk, and portions of Tehipite Canyon.

Clyde called back to Pablo, "The Obelisk over there on the left was first named Devil's Tombstone back in 1896. Later the US Geological Survey changed the name to the Obelisk, most likely around 1905. That's the rock I referred to before about the ill-fated rock climber. This ridge area we're on is referred to as Fin Dome. I've no idea when or where it got its name. The top has a granite outcropping that definitely looks like the dorsal fin of a fish."

Getting to the top edge, Clyde called back, "This is where we drop off down this switchback area to the exit stream of Geraldine Lakes."

Over the edge and out of site he went. The willows and brush were so thick, the trail wasn't visible, but Pablo's horse, Jay, knew the way and never missed a step, most of the time walking on top of the overlying brush. Down and down they went. The bottom was an inviting deep green meadow that looked closer than it really was. Finally getting out of the thicket and into the open meadow was a blessing. Across the greenery and up the granite they went, following the exit stream. At this point they encountered the hiking group, and all proceeded up to the lake. The group was glad to see Clyde as the trail was hard to follow up through the granite. In the brushy hillside, they simply piled off the side and got down any way they could. Just when the group thought the lake didn't exist, there it was. Lower Geraldine Lake was alive with jumping trout going after the massive amount of aquatic insects occupying the surface.

The hiking group caught up to the pack string just as unloading was about half done. Camp was to be set up on the far side of the lake. This was the only area large enough for this size group and provided natural shelter if bad weather came in.

With the unloading done and the empty packhorses still strung together, Clyde took the lead and motioned for Pablo to follow. This was after bidding farewell and confirming the return date in one week. Clyde started back to the main trail but turned right and up the canyon instead of back the way they came in. He turned back in the saddle and called to Pablo, "We're going to make a loop on our way back just so you can see different country. Coming up is a cross-country turnoff to, what I call, Middle Geraldine Lake. Won't take long. See. Just like I said, there it is. Let's go over on this side of the lake so I can show you something. Stop right here and just take a moment to look across the lake."

Pablo turned in the saddle, and the view took his breath away. He followed the water surface across the lake until it suddenly looked like all dropped off into oblivion. Nothing but sky and granite wall on the distant mountainside.

"Pablo, do you think humans invented the infinity pool? Nature has been making them for eons. This place is just off the trail far enough that few people know of its existence, and now you're one of 'em."

Clyde turned the string, headed back to the prior trail, and kept going up the canyon. He stopped at an inconspicuous gentle turn

Infinity Pool

in the trail. After getting off, he motioned for Pablo to do the same. They tied up and Clyde started to walk up the trail. "We are going up only a short distance to show you the reason why we're not staying on the trail through this part."

After only fifty yards, Pablo stopped in his tracks and couldn't believe where the trail went. It was up a sheer 70-degree pitch of rock. At most, there were finger- and toehold outcroppings of granite that would provide only modest leverage for hikers. This would be exceedingly dangerous for horses.

Clyde spoke up after letting Pablo think about it for about ten seconds. "What would be your options if you confronted this on your own?"

Pablo had to sit down, take his hat off, and stroke his chin in contemplation. "Well," he began, "I could disconnect each animal and lead them up, one at a time, and reassemble the string above this part, or I could simply loose-lead 'em up. But if they had top loads on their backs, any one of them could easily pitch over and cause a wreck. Or, I guess, I could unload everything and carry all the gear up myself and reload above the problem portion. But I don't see a safe tie-up place to reassemble the string. All and all, I think the best thing is to unsnap each animal, turn 180 degrees in place, resnap, and head back down the trail to a safe place and tie up. Then take my saddle horse and go scouting for an alternative route that would bring me back on the trail above this place."

"Attaboy," Clyde said after tapping his shoulder. "Often instead of powering your way through an obstacle, it's much smarter to broaden your vision and rethink it to find a smarter way. Going around is one of 'em. This goes for all things in life. Keep a focus on the end point, but how you get there often is variable. Learning to quickly adapt and act is the secret. Let's get back down to the horses, then you lead the way."

Pablo rode lead, going sidehill after crossing a small creek, then turning up following a relatively gentle slope. Keeping an eye on the problem portion of the trail, he then turned back toward the intended route. This required going over some flat granite that was rough and not glacially polished. Even with a 20-degree slope the horses had no problem with their footing. After a short distance, Pablo popped out on the trail again but above the troublesome area. Grinning, he turned back to Clyde.

"Perfect," Clyde said. "Now let's go back and get the string so we can get past this."

Up they rode until finally coming up to the totally rock-bound Upper Geraldine Lake. Clyde rode over to the opposite side of the exit stream and stopped to tie up. Pablo did the same. The pack string stayed behind Clyde's lead horse and stood perfectly still. After walking over to the campsite, Clyde sat down and motioned for Pablo to do the same.

"Pablo, see that granite dome over there. That's the Obelisk. That's the reason this group keeps coming up here almost every year. Back in 1953, the patriarch of the Hongola family was over toward the base of that rock just on a hike. His friend was a geologist. It didn't take long for the geologist to notice something different about several rocks in the area. He took several samples home to get 'em assayed and sure enough they were full of tungsten.

"They staked a claim and started mining three years later. The US government, in those days, would subsidize mining operations for minerals they deemed a necessity and wanted to stockpile. The Hongolas would haul the ore out on pack mules and horses, keeping the crew on-site. I guess the crew started complaining about wanting to get paid, but they had no way to get to town. The answer for Hongola was to have a small plane fly in and do a low pass, kicking out a sack with the miners' paychecks in it. The miners were then happy but still had to stay on the job since there was no way out. That made Hongola happy.

"I understand two of the miners were named Wild Bill and Little Bill. Wild Bill was never hard to locate after each winter. He usually had a room at the county jail. Little Bill was an exceptionally tough character. He survived the Bataan Death March, escaped, and could have come home since he was an American. Instead he stayed and spent the rest of the war as a guerrilla fighter with the Filipinos against the Japanese. All and all, I hear they didn't really take enough ore out to make it viable on its own, but with the subsidies, things worked out. When the government decided they had enough of a stockpile, the subsidies stopped and then so did the mine. The Hongolas kept up a small operation with their own labor, but soon the Forest Service took back the claim. That took place around 1992, during President Bush's administration. Since this area is in the Wilderness having a low-functioning mine within the boundaries didn't sit well. Anyway, the children of the mine founders have gone on and done well on their own.

"Most are retired now. One was an airline pilot and another a general surgeon. Good folks that grew up working hard and setting the course for success in their lives. There is still a rock monument as a claim marker so I'm sure this group, the Hongola family, will be over there tomorrow so they can take pictures and reconnect with their past."

Heading back down the trail with Clyde leading, Pablo soon turned at a nondescript fork in the trail and headed due west toward Spanish Mountain. The terrain began to change. The higher they went, the more the area began to look like high desert. The area was dry and rocky with clumps of purple sage, reminding Pablo of the high country back home in Mexico. He wondered maybe that's why it's called Spanish Mountain. Riding along, Pablo kept studying every corner of the hillsides, looking for evidence of the lost gold mine. He laughed at himself thinking if it was that easy to spot from the trail, no doubt someone would have discovered it by now.

Clyde and Pablo continued north and soon started a gradual descent. Noticing evidence of the previous Rough Fire, Clyde spoke up, "During the fire, Deb and Ms. McDougald, the US Forest Service packer I was talking about, had to ride this whole line and post stop signs at every turnoff in the trail. This was to keep the public from unknowingly traveling right into the fireline. With all the smoke, that wouldn't be hard to do. The air was totally thick with smoke, and breathing through a scarf was even difficult. With eyes burning, they could still see the bright glow of the fire coming through the smoke from up on the ridges above 'em. This was agonizing, knowing that at any time the wind could pick up and push the flames through the treetops overhead and trap them. By the end of the day, both of 'em were mighty glad to get that job done. It takes several days to get the smell of smoke off you, but sometimes that comes with the job.

"Later during the fire, Ms. McDougald had the task of packing in all the water pumps, hoses, and gasoline. The pumps were set up at each creek crossing, and the hoses stretched in both directions from there. This was necessary to act as a defensive tool when they set the backfires. Remember, all this was done with choking smoke, ash, and hot embers falling around her and the stock. Keeping all the animals calm and getting the job done under these conditions is not for the faint of heart. Folks don't really know just how dangerous these fires can be when you have to get up close and personal. Hopefully, a more commonsense approach to forest management will be followed in the near future. The entity that would benefit the most would be the forest itself."

The duo passed Spanish Lake and then the turnoff to Little Spanish Lake. Soon, they came out on a ridge overlooking a picture-postcard meadow with several log cabins at the tree line and a small creek meandering through the center.

Clyde stopped the string and, turning in the saddle, called back to Pablo. "Beautiful sight, isn't it? Not much has changed here for close to a hundred years. This place is called Statum Meadow. Named after a sheepman, A. H. Statham. The spelling has changed some. I hear he grazed this area starting back to nearly 1871. He went from here all the way back to Dinkey Creek. He also grazed in the canyon over along a creek that now has his name. This area later became a cow camp. Now it's owned by a group of four guys that belong to an organization called Back Country Horsemen. The person in the group I usually have contact with is an attorney from Visalia named Richard Cochran.

"The whole group seems quite nice and is respectful of the site. They've done much restoration and like to maintain the historical significance. You could do a painting of the site from here and put it on any Western calendar, and you would think it was done over a hundred years ago. Thanks to Mr. Cochran and his friends, it's the same place now as it was back then.

"A gal named Mary Piasecki has the cattle permit now. Her cow camp is down lower at the end of the road. That's another thing. You would be surprised down through history how many of the cattle outfits were owned and operated by women. Before Mary there was another lady named Bobbie Green. She had the outfit for about forty years. Historically, most of the women-owned operations were because the husband died and either the widow took over or sold out. Many of 'em stuck to it and did quite well. Nowadays, that's not usually the case. Mary got the cattle outfit all on her own.

"Keep that in mind. During your lifetime you'll have just as much, if not more, competition from women than men. I never thought that was a bad thing at all. The ladies bring a different perspective and tend to stay focused. Pablo, these traits can help you more than ya think. Picking a wife that shares the same goals as you is huge. With both of you rowing in the same direction, the sky is the limit as to what you can accomplish. Picking the right partner is the biggest decision you will ever make. I've known many men and women who picked wrong and did nothing but drag an anchor their whole lives. Don't be in any hurry. The right one will find you when you are ready. Keep your antennas out, though. You don't want to be caught sleeping when the right one comes along."

Soon the trailhead came into view. Dinkey and Patsy trotted up ahead and took up their usual position lying under the gooseneck trailer in the shade. After Clyde and Pablo unsaddled all the stock, they got all eleven horses to fit comfortably, nose to tail, in the trailer before they shut the gate. Clyde had already radioed Deb, letting her know how far out from headquarters they were. The last item on the list before departing was the command for the two dogs to load up. They promptly bolted out from under the trailer and easily jumped onto the pile of gear in the back of the flatbed. They soon found comfortable depressions and snuggled in for the short ride home.

Epilogue

Pablo could see the sun was about to rise but felt no rush to get up. This was the last morning of the summer he would wake up to see the dim light of early morning grace the golf-ball-size cones of the lodgepole pine outside his window. Summer was over, and school was to start Monday. Today was the last day to get down the hill and finish registering for his fall freshman classes at California State University, Fresno. No reason to change routine now, so he got up, dressed, and headed to the cookhouse for the usual cup of morning coffee.

Clyde was already there, relaxing in his recliner, feet up near the wood-burning stove. No trips were scheduled for today, which allowed for a rare day off. Pablo's mother was to arrive in about an hour to pick him up, and he wanted to be ready.

Not much was said as Pablo sat down to enjoy the morning fire and coffee. Both knew what the other was thinking. Mostly reflections on all the summer's trips with the amusements and education gained from the experiences. Pablo's belongings were all stored in one duffel bag that he had set on the front porch before entering. Pablo was proud that everything he owned was in the one bag. He reflected on what Clyde had told him several times throughout the summer. "If ya want to go far in this world, travel light." Clyde had reminded him of how good he felt when he finished his medical training in San Francisco and headed back to Clovis. Everything he owned easily fit into the trunk of his car. Clyde had often told him of not wasting hard-earned money on stupid stuff. It will soon become a burden, and ultimately you become its slave.

Within thirty minutes, Yolanda, Pablo's mother, drove in. With happy tears she was delighted to see her son again, remarking on how much weight he had lost but how now he was solid muscle. Clyde and Yolanda exchanged a hug that was followed by a prolonged, mother-to-mother hug with Deb. Both women knew this was the end of a chapter in Pablo's life and the start of a new one. Clyde and Deb invited Pablo to come back and work next summer and Pablo said he would be delighted and promised to do just that.

Mother and son got into the car and slowly drove off. The four kept waving until the vehicle turned the corner and was lost behind the trees.

On the drive down, Pablo reflected on what Clyde had told him late in the summer. "After you've been gone for almost three months, ya might as well have been on the moon. When you go back, all your old friends will have changed in your eyes. Their thought processes and focus will be the same as when you left. You, however, will have changed dramatically. Soon you will spend less and less time with them and focus on your own path. That's called personal growth. You have to experience this before you fully understand, and you will."

That afternoon, sitting at the registration table at Fresno State, Pablo completed the remaining portions of class registration. During the drive through town, the familiar surroundings had looked the same but felt foreign to him. He paused at the last box to be filled in. It was labeled Declared Major. He had given this much thought over the summer and even more so toward the end. Taking a deep breath and holding the pen with a firm hand, he wrote "Pre-Med" without hesitation.

Index

About the Author

Deb and Allen Clyde. *Photo courtesy of C. Howard Stimmel.*

Dr. Allen Clyde has operated a horse-packing service in the John Muir Wilderness for forty years, transporting over twenty thousand visitors and their supplies. He is also a podiatric physician and surgeon. Dr. Clyde has served on the Fresno County (California) Board of Education for nearly twenty years. He lives in Clovis, California. *Life Lessons on the Sierra Trail* is his first book.

About the Illustrator

Claudia Fletcher. *Photo courtesy of author.*

Professional artist and muralist **Claudia Fletcher**, born and raised on a cotton and alfalfa farm in Madera, California, possesses an inherent love for the San Joaquin Valley and a natural talent for capturing its essence through art. Following in the footsteps of her artist grandmother, Fletcher was only eight years old when she participated in her first art show. She has won many art competitions; produced commissioned artwork, portrait paintings, and drawings for clients across the United States; and created murals for several cities. Since 1992, Fletcher has painted the official poster for the annual Clovis Rodeo. Referring to her favorite art subject, Fletcher says, "The power and magnificence of the horse was my first channel for the expression of my talent in drawing and painting."

CPSIA information can be obtained
at www.ICGtesting.com
Printed in the USA
JSHW030755121020
8612JS00004B/4

9 780941 936040